# CULTURE

# AND

# INTERCULTURAL DIALOGUE

# CULTURE

# AND
# INTERCULTURAL DIALOGUE

J. Kuruvachira

CreateSpace

J. Kuruvachira, *Culture and Intercultural Dialogue*, Rome, CreateSpace, 2018

ISBN-13: 978-1983434266

ISBN-10:1983434264

**Cover design and layout**: Noble Kollithanathu

**Subject References**:
Culture
Cultural Pluralism
Cultural Integration
Cultural Pluralism and Catholic Church
Intercultural Dialogue
Intercultural Education
Intercultural Dialogue and Catholic Church

# CONTENTS



## Chapter 1

## MEANING AND CHARACTERISTICS OF CULTURE

### Some basic concepts and related issues

Introduction

# Chapter 2
## INTERCULTURAL DIALOGUE
### Meaning, Aims, Conditions and Forms

# INTRODUCTION

Two topics widely discussed today by scholars, educational institutions, national and international organisations and governments are "culture" and "intercultural dialogue". Since Vatican Council II, the Catholic Church is also actively involved in the study of cultures and the promotion of intercultural dialogue.

Culture is part of the identity of people and it lends them a sense of belonging and uniqueness. There are a great variety of cultures in the world. They are part of the rich patrimony of the world, and whatever is true, good and noble in them are to be preserved and passed on to future generations.

Today, more than ever, people are aware of the fact of cultural pluralism. There are many ways of responding to pluralism of cultures. It can range from co-existence of cultures without integration, assimilation of minority cultures by dominant ones, oppression, political manipulation and violent opposition to cultures different from one's own to mutual acceptance, dialogue and integration of cultures. Our privileged way to respond is with acceptance, dialogue and integration of cultures for mutual enrichment.

This brief study intends to provide a simple, concise and preliminary understanding of the concept of culture and intercultural dialogue. It is divided into two chapters. The first chapter discusses the meaning and characteristics of culture, some basic concepts connected with it, factors contributing to cultural pluralism, some negative attitudes towards cultural pluralism, and three basic approaches to culture: relativistic, assimilative and intercultural. The second chapter deals with the nature, necessity, conditions and aims of intercultural dialogue, theological and anthropological foundations for it, various forms of intercultural dialogue, the importance of intercultural education, challenges to intercultural dialogue and the attitude of the Catholic Church towards intercultural dialogue.

This study is carried out from a Catholic perspective. Therefore, references are made to some of the Catholic Church's documents on culture and intercultural dialogue and the magisterium of Popes, especially John Paul II and Benedict XVI. Mainly four important documents were used to prepare this booklet: "Towards a Pastoral approach to Culture" (1999) by the Vatican Pontifical Council for Culture, the "UNESCO Convention on the Protection and promotion of the Diversity of Cultural Expressions" (2005), "White Paper on Intercultural Dialogue" (2008) by the Council of Europe, and "Educating to Intercultural Dialogue in Catholic Schools. Living in Harmony for a Civilization of Love" (2013) by the Holy See's Congregation for Catholic Education.

It is hoped that this short study can serve as a handbook on culture and intercultural dialogue for university students, educators from all walks of life, religious leaders as well as those engaged in the promotion of intercultural dialogue in civil society.

Finally, I am grateful to Julia Perry for doing the linguistic and stylistic corrections and the proofreading.

J. Kuruvachira

Rome, 7 April 2018

Chapter 1

# MEANING AND CHARACTERISTICS OF CULTURE

## Some basic concepts and related issues

## Introduction

We are living in a world in which there is greater awareness and experience of cultural pluralism than in the past. Today people of different cultures are increasingly interacting with each other and as a consequence, societies around the world are rapidly changing and becoming pluralistic. The accelerated pace of globalisation and the influence of mass media make it possible for people of different cultures to be in close contact. Today, culture is the main focus of sociologists, anthropologists, ethnologists, historians, governments, social developmental programmes, political movements, human rights activists, media, and organisations that promote ethnic consciousness and cultural identity. It has been argued by many scholars that the 21st century will be multicultural and so the world must learn to accept and live with it. However, whether these cultural interactions and consequent radical social changes are positive or negative will depend a great deal on the attitudes which people have towards other cultural groups, and the level of sensitivity and respect they have for cultural values. Dialogue between cultures is one of the oldest, most basic human ways of interaction between peoples, and it serves as an antidote to cultural conflicts, and enables them to live together in peace and develop a sense of community and belonging, in order to build a world society founded on peace, justice, harmony, mutual acceptance and collaboration.

## 1. Meaning of culture

It is not easy to define culture. Yet there are numerous definitions for it. Though various schools of thought and scholars have offered a variety of definitions, there is no single definition that encompasses all the meanings attached to it. However, there seems to be a general consensus that culture is the most unique characteristic of *homo sapiens*, and that it distinguishes them from animals. The famous anthropologist Melville J. Herskovits says: "What marks off man, the social animal of our concern, from all of these [animals], is *culture*."[1] Culture is also recognised as a factor, which is at the core of individual and social identity. Below are some definitions of culture, which when taken together, can give us a general idea of what is meant by culture:

1) Culture is that complex whole which includes knowledge, beliefs, art, morals, laws, custom, and any other capabilities and habits acquired by human beings as a

---

[1] Melville J. Herskovits, *Man and His Works. The Science of Cultural Anthropology*, New York, Alfred A. Knopf, 1964, p. 17. (Italics in the original)

member of society.[2] (Edward Burnett Tylor)

2) Culture is the way of life of people. It consists of conventional patterns of thought and behaviour, including values, beliefs, rules of conduct, political organisation, economic activity, and the like, which are passed on from one generation to the next by learning and not by biological inheritance.[3] (Elvin Hatch)

3) Culture is all that which is non-biological and socially transmitted, including artistic, social, ideological and religious patterns of behaviour and the technology of mastering the environment.[4] (Charles Winick)

4) Culture is the lifeline of a human community. It is a basic determinant of social behaviour. It consists of social and religious structures, intellectual and artistic manifestations that characterise a society.[5] (John Friedl)

5) Culture refers to the complex, changing nexus of values, attitudes, beliefs, practices, traditions, social institutions and so on of a community; it also includes religion, language, foods, history, dress and so on.[6]

6) Culture implies the totality of factors by which the communal life of people within a society is made meaningful and significant. They include religion, social and intellectual values, science, the arts, education, and the image, which every individual has of himself or herself as part of the

---

[2] Cf. Edward. B. Tylor, *Primitive Culture* [1874], New York, Gordon Press, 2nd edition, 1977, p. 1.

[3] Cf. Elvin Hatch, "Culture", in *The Social Science Encyclopedia*, Adam Kuper and Jessica Kuper (eds.), London, Routledge, 1985, p. 178.

[4] Cf. Charles Winick, *Dictionary of Anthropology*, London, Peter Owen, n.d, p. 144.

[5] Cf. John Friedl, *Cultural Anthropology*, New York, Joanna Cotler Books, 1976, p. 53.

[6] Cf. Paola A. Cordeiro, Timothy G. Reagan and Linda P Martinez, *Multiculturalism and TQE. Addressing Cultural Diversity in Schools*, California, Corwin Press, 1994, p. 20.

system.[7]

7) The word "culture" in its general sense indicates everything whereby man develops and perfects his many bodily and spiritual qualities.[8] (*Gaudium et spes*)

8) Culture is the particular expression of human beings, their specific way of being and organising their presence in the world.[9] (Congregation for Catholic Education)

9) Culture is the total manner in which a human society responds to an environment.[10] (Thomas Menamparampil)

Thus we see that culture is a very complex concept which encompasses everything that is related to a human group: beliefs, customs, traditions, practices, attitudes, values, norms, ideas, artefacts, signs, symbols and behaviour patterns. It is the environment in which a human being lives and grows. It is the totality of human experiences acquired, inherited, shared and transmitted. Culture covers the material and the spiritual, the mundane and the transcendent as well as science, technology, education, aesthetics, oral traditions, literature, social structures, value systems, institutions, social norms, thought patterns, worldviews, emotional traits and psychological peculiarities of a human group. These elements when combined define culture.

## 2. Characteristics of culture

Culture is the worldview and life style of a social group. It

---

[7] Cf. *Human Rights in the Intercultural Dialogue*, Cologne, Konrad Adenauer Foundation, 1998, p. 21.

[8] Cf. Vatican Council II, Pastoral Constitution *Gaudium et spes* (7 December 1965), in *Acta Apostolicae Sedis,* 58 (1966), no. 53.

[9] Cf. Congregation for Catholic Education, *Educating to intercultural dialogue in catholic schools: living in harmony for a civilization of love,* Città del Vaticano, Libreria Editrice Vaticana, 2013, no. 1.

[10] Cf. Thomas Menamparampil, *The Challenge of Cultures*, Bombay, St. Pauls, 1996, p. 9.

has certain basic characteristics. The following can be identified as the principal ones:

## 2.1. All human beings have culture

All human beings are cultural beings. It is integral to the identity of a human person. Culture combines many elements to create a unique way of living for a human group. The culture of a person is acquired, learned and shared socially rather than inherited biologically. In this sense it is not an individual phenomenon but a product of society, and is transmitted from one generation to the next. Although all people have culture, the manifestation of each culture is unique. Cultural rootlessness, which has so many causes, shows how important cultural roots are. It contributes to people's social and cultural identity and dignity.[11] Today the general tendency among people is to affirm cultural diversity, appreciate their distinctiveness and preserve and enhance all that is true, good and noble in them and learn from them. Human beings have taken many centuries to arrive at this mature and positive way of dealing with cultural diversity. However, this does not mean that today all cultures in all parts of the world enjoy the recognition and affirmation they deserve. In fact, there are many cultures that struggle to survive and define their identity in the world. Many cultures have also "disappeared" from the face of earth. However, in general the situation has become much more positive than what it used to be until some centuries ago.

## 2.2. Human beings as producers of culture

Culture exists only through human beings and for human

---

[11] Cf. Pontifical Council for Culture, *Towards a Pastoral Approach to Culture,* Città del Vaticano, Libraria Editrice Vaticana, 1999, no. 8.

beings. It exists from the time of *homo sapiens*[12] because human beings are the only animals that create and use culture in the true sense of the term, and therefore they can be called "cultural animals".[13] In fact, human beings are spoken of as "culture-building animals".[14] Culture is the product of human creativity. It is the collective product of human experience, and shared interpretations of that experience as communicated within specific groups. Culture is the whole of human activity, human intelligence and emotions, and the human quest for meaning in life as well as human customs and ethics. Culture is so natural to man that human nature can only be revealed through culture.[15] Culture is not the product of individual human beings but of a human society. In this sense, culture is social and is shared. But culture and society are not the same thing. Cultural expressions and symbols are taught and learned and passed on from one generation to another, and each generation adds something of its own to the existing culture. Culture is accumulative in the sense that it adds new traits to the existing ones and borrows from others and absorbs them as one's own. A social group can also decide to reject certain previous cultural patterns in the course of evolution. Culture is a powerful human tool for the survival of a group. All people are part of a culture, depend upon it and shape it. Thus as Pope John Paul II says: "Human beings are both child and parent of the culture in which they

---

[12] Cf. Hervé Carrier, *Dizionario della Cultura. Per l'analisi culturale e l'inculturazione*, Città del Vaticano, Libreria Editrice Vaticana, 1997, p. 121.

[13] There is a difference of opinion in the behavioural sciences about whether or not human beings are the only animals that create and use culture. The answer to this problem depends on how narrow or broad culture is defined. Some claims that many other animal species teach their young what they themselves learned in order to survive. Cf. http://anthro.palomar.edu/culture/culture_1.htm (20.5.2017)

[14] Cf. Melville J. Herskovits, *Man and His Works,* p. 18.

[15] Cf. Pontifical Council for Culture, *Towards a Pastoral Approach to Culture,* no. 2.

are immersed."[16]

## 2.3. Plurality of cultures

A plurality of cultures exists in the world. This is because cultures vary from society to society, and every culture is unique in its own way and specific to a human group. Different styles of life and multiple scales of values arise from the diverse manner of using things, expressing oneself, practicing religion, forming customs, establishing laws and juridical institutions and cultivating the sciences, the arts and beauty.[17] Increased interaction between peoples and nations, mass media and social communication, research studies, extensive travels, tourism, activities of national and international cultural organisations, cultural exchange programmes, greater awareness of the limitations of one's own culture and an attitude of learning from others, and so on, have played a major role in arriving at the awareness and recognition of the fact of cultural pluralism.

## 2.4. Culture has coherence

Culture is the distinctive sign of a society, social group and human community. It is organised, has coherence and structure among the patterns of human behaviour, and makes sense for those who live in accordance with it. It exhibits regularities that permit its analysis by the methods of science. When culture is closely analysed, we find but a series of patterned reactions that characterise the behaviour of the individuals who constitute a given group.[18] This aspect spontaneously distinguishes one group from another and indicates the uniqueness and identity of each culture. Because

---

[16] John Paul II, Encyclical Letter *Fides et ratio* (14 September 1998), in *Acta Apostolicae Sedis,* 91 (1999), no. 71.

[17] Cf. *Gaudium et spes,* no. 53.

[18] Cf. Melville J. Herskovits, *Man and His Works,* pp. 27-28, 625.

of this, one can identify different types of culture, and speak for example of the culture of Christianity, the culture of Islam the culture of Europe, the culture of Asia, the culture of workers, the culture of immigrants, rural culture, city culture, the culture of young people, family culture, clan and tribal culture, etc.

## 2.5. Culture as both stable and dynamic

Culture is *both* stable and ever-changing.[19] Cultural change is viewed in terms of modifications of the cultural systems and subsystems and not merely as the addition, loss or modification of cultural elements that are superficial. Since cultures are inseparable from people and their history, they share the changing conditions of the world. Hence a simple, homogenous and unchanging culture does not exist. But all cultures do not change at the same pace and in the same way. At times cultural changes are resisted by certain sections of people in the name of the so-called preservation of cultures in their "pristine purity", which in reality is only a utopia. Among the many factors responsible for cultural change, the State, civil society, political and economic factors, attitudes towards religious beliefs and encounter with other cultures are considered to be the main ones.

Cultural dynamism moves in two directions: on the one hand, there is a tendency towards greater cultural uniformity; on the other hand, the uniqueness and specific nature of cultures are exalted. It is to be seen what will be the future of the specific identity of each culture, given the pressures of human migration, mass communication, social networks and, above all, the enormous expansion of customs and products resulting in a "westernisation" of the world. However, although the inevitable tendency to cultural uniformity remains strong, there are also many elements, alive and

---

[19] Cf. Ibid., p. 20.

active, of variation and distinction between groups. These often provoke reactions of fundamentalism and the self-referential closing in on oneself. Thus pluralism and the variety of traditions, customs and languages, which of their nature produce mutual enrichment and development, can lead to an exaggeration of individual identity flaring up into clashes and conflicts.[20]

## 2.6. No culture is absolute

Strictly speaking there is no universal culture as such because every culture is particular and unique. Consequently, no culture is absolute, and every culture has limitations and is therefore finite. Cultural absolutism upholds the exclusiveness of a culture and considers it alone as the absolute standard for everything. It is a sign of a false sense of superiority of a culture over others, and is in danger of extinction sooner or later. Cultural absolutism can also lead to ethnocentrism, which is a tendency to judge and interpret other cultures according to the criterion of one's own culture. Awareness of this fact normally leads people of one culture to be open to other cultures. Thus they welcome people from different cultures, live together, work together and enrich each other and create an intercultural open society. It is said that one understands one's own culture better by watching alternative expressions in another culture.[21]

## 2.7. Culture is not the same as civilisation

Culture is not to be equated with civilisation[22] understood

---

[20] Cf. Congregation for Catholic Education, *Educating to intercultural dialogue in catholic schools*, no 4

[21] Cf. Thomas Menamparampil, *The Challenge of Cultures*, p. 19.

[22] In the past sometimes civilisation was used as a substitute for culture. In England and France the term "civilisation" was used in preference to culture. Civilisation implied a "high" culture characterized by writing and highly developed political system. In America culture and civilisation were

as refinement in human behaviour, advanced stages of social development, technology and organization. Culture is subjective. There is no universally accepted measure for refinement, advancement or organisation. Each culture has its own internal logic and norms with which they measure refinement, development and correct forms of behaviour. Customs differ, habits change and we cannot call anyone uncultured or lacking in culture or call a culture high or low, superior or inferior, primitive or advanced. Every culture is the result of a continuous mixing of populations or the hybridisation of the human family in the course of its history. This means that there is no such thing as a "pure" culture.[23] In the same way, we cannot call anyone uncivilised. Even the so-called primitive people had their own civilisation. Nevertheless, culture and civilisation are interconnected. Hervé Carrier opines that culture represents the soul of a collectivity while civilisation is built on science, technology, and may correspond to material progress. Hence culture is the spirit of a people, and civilisation constitutes its external works.[24]

## 2.8. Culture and language

There is an intimate relationship between culture and language. Language is the most human of all abilities. It is one of the defining characteristics of *homo sapiens*. Wherever human beings exist, language exists.[25] Language is a system of signs, verbal or otherwise, intended for communication. It

---

interchangeably used by European writers. Cf. G. O. Lang, "Culture", in *New Catholic Encyclopedia*, Vol. 4, Washington, Thomson and Gale, 2nd edition, 2003, p. 427.

[23] Cf. Congregation for Catholic Education, *Educating to intercultural dialogue in catholic schools*, no. 3.

[24] Cf. Hervé Carrier, *Dizionario della Cultura*, pp. 92-93.

[25] Cf. Victoria A. Fromkin, "Language", in *The Social Science Encyclopedia*, Adam Kuper and Jessica Kuper (eds.), London, Routledge, 1985, p. 442.

is the most elaborate symbol systems of humankind.

Language is one of the most universal and diverse forms of expression of human culture. Joshua A. Fishman argues that there are three major ways in which language is related to culture: a) language itself is a major and crucial *part* of culture; b) every language provides an *index* of the culture with which it is most intimately associated (i.e. it provides the lexical terms for the bulk of the artefacts, concerns, values, and behaviours recognised by their associated cultures); c) every language becomes *symbolic* of the culture with which it is most intimately associated.[26]

Languages result from a historical and collective experience and express culturally specific worldviews and value systems. Linguistic diversity is a clear reflection of cultural diversity, and language issues are central to culture. Language is a tool to maintain and communicate cultural expressions, cultural thoughts and cultural ties. Hence language is at the heart of issues of cultural identity. For this reason, it is said that learning a new language involves learning a new culture.

## 2.9. Culture and religion

Religion and culture are intrinsically related. Religion, in one way or another, influences all the aspects of cultural life, and religion in turn is influenced by culture. Religion can be said to represent the transcendent dimension of culture and in a certain way its soul. A religious faith is always lived within a culture.[27] Religion is sometimes a central element of

---

[26] Cf. Joshua A. Fishman, "Language and Culture", in *The Social Science Encyclopedia*, Adam Kuper and Jessica Kuper (eds.), London, Routledge, 1985, p. 444.

[27] Cf. *Insegnamenti di Benedetto XVI*, Vol. V parte 1, Vatican City, Libraria Editrice Vaticana, 2010, p. 791.

culture.[28] In many indigenous populations, for example, culture is essentially an expression of religious beliefs. But culture is broader than religion. On the one hand the history of religion shows that a community of believers proceeds by degrees of faithfulness to God, drawing from and shaping the culture it meets.[29] On the other hand religions have certainly contributed to the progress of cultures and the construction of a more humane society.

Pope John Paul II said that religion has the power to shape cultures. On 31 January 2002 he said at the University of Roma Tre, Rome, "Religion is important for the formation of cultures. It is enough to look at history with objectivity to realise how important religion has been in the formation of cultures, and how with its influence it has shaped the entire human *habitat*. To ignore or deny this is not only an error of perspective, but also a disservice to the truth about the human person."[30] He also acknowledged that religions can became cultures. He considered Christianity, Judaism and Islam to be world religions and , also as cultures. On 24 February 2000 in his address to His Excellency Mohammed Sayed Tantawi grand Sheikh of Al-Azhar the pope said: "There is a strict connection between religions, religious faith and culture. Islam is a religion. Christianity is a religion. Islam has become a culture. Christianity has become also a culture."[31] Religions can also be influenced by cultures; they can take ideas from cultures to express themselves. For example, right from the early times, Christianity learned to express the truth of Christ through the help of ideas and according to the

---

[28] This view does not consider the fact that there could also be non-religious cultures. At the same time this does not rule out the fact that some kind of belief-system may be involved in even in such cultures.

[29] Cf. *Insegnamenti di Benedetto XVI,* Vol. V parte 1, p. 791.

[30] *Insegnamenti di Giovanni Paolo II*, Vol. XXV parte 1, Città del Vaticano, Libreria Editrice Vaticana, 2004, p. 146.

[31] *Insegnamenti di Giovanni Paolo II*, Vol. XXIII parte 1, Città del Vaticano, Libreria Editrice Vaticana, 2002, p. 252.

cultures of the various peoples and nations.[32]

According to Pope Benedict XVI, religion and culture as interrelated expressions of the deepest spiritual aspirations of our common humanity, naturally serve as incentives for dialogue and co-operation between peoples in the service of peace and genuine development.[33] It also serves as a foundation for cultural initiatives on a wide range of levels and for genuine dialogue of cultures and religions.[34] He stated further that genuine adherence to religion far from narrowing our minds, widens the horizon of human understanding. It protects civil society from the excesses of the unbridled ego which tend to absolutise the finite and eclipse the infinite; it ensures that freedom is exercised hand in hand with truth, and it adorns culture with insights concerning all that is true, good and beautiful.[35] Thus culture serves as a solid foundation for intercultural dialogue in interreligious relations.

Today in some societies secularisation is an alarming reality. Even if the institutionalised religions undergo cultural regression, religion will not disappear from modern society as is clear from the affirmation of new religious movements and cults and the emergence of the sacred even in advanced industrialised societies.[36] This means that religion is still a cultural phenomenon *par excellence*.

## 2.10. Secularised cultures

Secularisation refers to the *decline* of religion inasmuch as values, doctrines and religious institutions which once

---

[32] Cf. *Insegnamenti di Giovanni Paolo II*, Vol. IV parte 1, *Insegnamenti di Giovanni Paolo II*, Vol. IV parte 1, Città del Vaticano, Libreria Editrice Vaticana, 1981, p. 385.

[33] Cf. *Insegnamenti di Benedetto XVI*, Vol. VI part 1, Città del Vaticano, Libraria Editrice Vaticana, 2011, p. 744.

[34] Cf. *Insegnamenti di Benedetto XVI*, Vol. V parte 1, pp. 791-792.

[35] Cf. Ibid., p. 763.

[36] Cf. Hervé Carrier, *Dizionario della Cultura*, p. 336.

characterised the society are constantly losing their status and their influence; it means *de-sacralisation* of the world, *lack of involvement* of society in religion[37] and real *privatisation* of religious sentiments.[38] Today secularisation is a worldwide phenomenon, and in most advanced societies it permeates the whole social structure and affects the life of the masses and public life so that one can speak of a secularised culture.[39] Western society has an accelerating process of secularisation, with the danger of an extreme marginalisation of religious experience, seen as only being legitimate within the private sphere. More generally, in the dominant mind-set, the anthropological question is quietly eliminated, i.e. the question about the full dignity and destiny of human beings. Thus in secularisation the aim pursued is eradicating all

---

[37] Cf. L. Dani ed E. Roggero, "Secolarizzazione", in *Nuovo Dizionario di Sociologia,* Franco Demarchi, Aldo Ellena e Bernardo Cattarinussi (a cura di), Milano, Edizioni Paoline, 1987, pp. 1825-1826.

[38] Cf. Hervé Carrier, *Dizionario della Cultura*, p. 336.

[39] Some scholars argue that there is no real secularisation process taking place in the world. For example, Peter Berger says: "[…] the assumption that we live in a secularised world is false: The world today, with some exceptions […] is as furiously religious as it ever was, and in some places more so than ever." Peter L. Berger, "The Desecularisation of the World: A Global Overview", in *The Desecularisation of the World. Religion and World Politics,* Peter L. Berger (ed.), Washington, Ethics and Public Policy Centre, 1999, p. 2. Again, it is argued that despite the rapid "de-Christianisation" of Europe the late twentieth century witnessed a dramatic resurgence of religion in many other parts of the world. The rise of "Islamic fundamentalism", "Hindu fundamentalism", various forms of religious nationalism, Christian Pentecostalism, emergence of neo-paganism, eclectic and mystical spiritual beliefs and practices associated with the New Age movement and Eastern religions, have been identified as signs of the revival of religious culture. The International Theological Commission of the Catholic Church affirms the same reality. It says: "Despite secularisation, the religious sense of the people of our time has not disappeared." International Theological Commission, "Christianity and the World Religions", in *Texts and Documents 1986-2007*, Vol. II, Michael Sharkey and Thomas Weinandy (eds.), San Francisco, Ignatius Press, 2009, no. 2, p. 146.

religious expression from culture.[40]

## 2.11. Common elements in cultures

In spite of the plurality of cultures, upon closer examination one can trace many common elements in them. Cultures are profoundly dynamic and they undergo changes in time. Nevertheless, beneath their more superficial changes, they show significant common elements. Cultural diversity should therefore be understood within the broader horizon of the *unity of the human race*, in the light of which one can grasp the profound meaning of the very differences, instead of the radicalisation of identity, which makes cultures resistant to any beneficial influence from the outside.[41] One can trace such common elements in cultures as the following: values and beliefs, ethical norms and laws, religion, language and symbols, customs and traditions, arts and literature, social organisation, technology, education, forms of government, economic systems, aspirations, etc.[42] These elements constitute a path for dialogue between cultures. At the same time the complexity of a culture cannot be understood or evaluated without reference to culture as a whole. Hence viewing culture in its totality as an integrated unity is important.

---

[40] Cf. Congregation for Catholic Education, *Educating to intercultural dialogue in catholic schools*, no. 9.

[41] Cf. John Paul II, *"Dialogo tra le culture per una civiltà dell'amore e della pace"*, Messaggio per la celebrazione delle Giornata mondiale della pace (8 dicembre 2000), in *Insegnamenti di Giovanni Paolo II*, Vol. XXIII, parte 2, Città del Vaticano, Libraria Editrice Vaticana, 2002, nos. 7, 9.

[42] In order to discover the common elements in cultures, it is enough to study and compare, for example, the legends, oral traditions, sacred scriptures, proverbs, myths, narratives, oral and written laws, etc., of different cultures. Hervé Carrier states that anthologists have identified seven principal common cultural elements which are the typical characteristic of a culture: technology, economic organisation, social organisation, political organisation, education, religion, and cultural symbols. Cf. Hervé Carrier, *Dizionario della Cultura*, p. 412.

## 2.12. Human nature transcends cultures

Human beings always exist in a particular culture. However, a human person is not exhaustively defined by that same culture. The very progress of cultures demonstrates that there is something in human beings, which transcends those cultures. This "something" is precisely *human nature*. Every culture with its inner capacity gives expression to the *one* human nature. [43] This nature is itself the measure of culture and the condition of ensuring that a human being does not become prisoner to any of his culture, but asserts his personal dignity by living in accordance with the profound truth of his being.[44] Every culture with its inner capacity to give and receive, gives expression to one human nature. Yet the individual is never expressed through his or her own culture, but transcends it in the constant search for something beyond.[45]

## 3. Some basic terms connected with culture

Since culture is a complex reality, it is important to know what certain terms signify so that one's discourse about it becomes more precise and accurate. Below are explanations of some basic concepts which frequently occur in discussions about culture and a familiarity with them can greatly enhance one's understanding of it.

## 3.1 Cultural Pluralism

Cultural pluralism is an approach, which favours a particularistic outlook to cultures and stresses the need for the

---

[43] It is to be noted that there are some scholars and schools of thought that deny the existence of a universal human nature.

[44] Cf. John Paul II, Encyclical Letter *Veritatis splendor* (6 August 1993), in *Acta Apostolicae Sedis,* 85 (1993), no. 53.

[45] Cf. *Insegnamenti di Benedetto XVI,* Vol. V parte 1, p. 791.

careful and holistic study of each culture's unique features because each culture possesses its own rationality and coherence in terms of which its customs and beliefs are to be interpreted.[46] Cultural pluralism is a typical tendency of modern societies. It allows individual ethnic groups to have a right to exist on their own terms within the larger society while retaining their unique cultural identities, values and practices. In the context of cultural pluralism there is always a *dominant culture*. Often cultural pluralism is the result of refusing to be assimilated by another culture or not being allowed to assimilate into the dominant culture.

Cultural pluralism has positive and negative aspects. *Positively*, it allows cultural co-existence, cultural diversity and mutual respect. It negates totalitarian ideologies and every form of irrational violence and allows for a free society. Thus it becomes a wide community consisting of many small communities, which enrich each other with their specific gifts. There is an attitude of openness, tolerance and mutual respect. It promotes democracy, solidarity, and liberty to defend one's cultural values through legitimate means. *Negatively* cultural pluralism can mean passivity and indifference towards other cultures. In the name of cultural pluralism one can turn out to be a person of "single dimension". Contradicting activities and conflicting truths can co-exist in indifference. This can be a characteristic of materialistic cultures that are closed to the spiritual dimension. This type of pluralism is a threat to many cultures in the industrialised world.[47]

## 3.2. Multiculturalism

Multiculturalism refers to the co-existence of many ethnic groups in the same community with diverse cultural

---

[46] Cf. Charlotte Seymour-Smith, *Macmillan Dictionary of Anthropology*, London, MacMillan, 1986, p. 64.

[47] Cf. Hervé Carrier, *Dizionario della Cultura*, pp. 312-314.

expressions.[48] It not only refers to elements of ethnic or national culture, but also includes linguistic, religious and socio-economic diversity. It means the preservation of different cultures or cultural identities within a unified society, as a State or nation. It is the outcome of globalisation, migration and media culture. Multiculturalism *lacks the requirement of a dominant culture*. When multiculturalism becomes the official policy of a nation it ensures that all citizens can keep their identities, can take pride in their ancestry and have a sense of belonging. This gives people a feeling of security and self-confidence, making them more open to, and accepting of, diverse cultures. Multiculturalism encourages racial and ethnic harmony and cross-cultural understanding. It calls for living with differences. It is an immense resource for mutual enrichment and at the same time a great challenge and threat.

Multiculturalism has been strongly *criticised* in recent years, both in the academic literature and in the political sphere, mainly because it generates cultural relativism. Multiculturalism emphasises the distinctiveness of ethnic, cultural and religious minorities. Consequently it implies a static and substantially immutable cultural situation.[49] Critics of multiculturalism question the ideal of the maintenance of distinct ethnic cultures within a State. Today countries that once embraced multiculturalism are abandoning it. Some countries aspire to an assimilationist approach to deal with multiculturalism. They make learning the norms and values of the host society mandatory for immigrants. Critics of multiculturalism may *argue against* different ethnic and cultural groups assimilating to the existing laws and values of the country. Alternatively, critics may *argue for* the assimilation of different ethnic and cultural groups to a single

---

[48] Cf. Giuliana Gennai, *Lessico Interculturale*, Bologna, Editrice Missionaria Italiana, 2005, p. 114.

[49] Cf. Ibid., p. 81,

national identity. Multiculturalism is a particular subject of debate in certain European nations that were once associated with a single, national cultural ethos.

## 3.3. Multiethnicity

Ethnicity refers to the collective identity of individuals who belong to a particular community or nationality. The members of an ethnic group consider themselves distinct from others because of their culture, language, history, ancestry, religion, symbols, traditions, etc.[50] Multiethnicity (Polyethnicity)[51] refers to co-existence between people from different ethnic backgrounds within a country or other specific geographic region. They share a real or presumed common origin, same name, symbols, history, values, traditions, and manifest solidarity among themselves. They make distinctions between "insider" and outsider, "we" and "they". Multiethnicity occurs when multiple ethnicities inhabit a given area, specifically through means of immigration, intermarriage, trade and conquest and post-war land-divisions.

Multiethnicity has been *criticised* on the ground that it divides nations and complicates politics as local and national governments attempt to satisfy all ethnic groups. Multiethnicity can lead to ethnic conflicts and negatively affect national integration and unity. Often it is orchestrated

---

[50] Cf. Anna Maria Fantauzzi, "Razzismo biologico, razzismo differenzialista?", in *Razzismo, xenofobia, esclusione sociale*, Aurelio Angelini (a cura di), Roma, MMXIV Aracne editrice, 2014, p. 150; Giuliana Gennai, *Lessico Interculturale*, pp. 55-57.

[51] A distinction needs to be made between multiethnicity and multiculturalism because they mean two different things. Ethnicity primarily refers to group *identity* arising from a common history, kinship and language. Culture refers to the way members of a particular ethnic group relate to their environment and each other. Culture includes legends, laws, structures, values, customs and artifacts and worldviews. In this sense culture is more complex than ethnicity.

by political and social groups for obtaining political mileage. Critics of multiethnicity point out that ethnic violence is on the increase. In addition, the quest for group, ethnic or national identity is becoming more relentless as the stranger and those who are different are rejected to such a degree that at times barbarous acts are committed against them. Sometimes it leads to ethnic or nationalistic wars, racist massacres or "ethnic cleansing". In other situations it gravely compromises the equal dignity of every human person.

## 3.4. Interculturality

Interculturality is a concept, which refers to the evolving relationship between different cultural groups. It is defined as the existence and equitable interaction of diverse cultures and the possibility of generating shared cultural expressions through dialogue and mutual respect.[52] It explicitly recognises the value of cultural diversity while positively promoting interaction, mixing, dialogue, reciprocity, collaboration and hybridisation between cultural groups. Interculturality derives from the understanding that cultures prosper only in contact with other cultures, not in isolation, and that cultures can influence each other. It recognises strongly the need to enable each culture to survive and flourish, but highlights also the right of all cultures to contribute to the cultural landscape of the society in which they are present. Interculturality is becoming increasingly important in the modern world as more and more people migrate from one country to another to escape from war, conflict, persecution or poverty, or to reunite families. Interculturality has benefits, including cultural enrichment and creativity.

Interculturality has been *criticised* by some because when two groups of people meet whose cultures differ significantly

---

[52] Cf. *UNESCO Convention on the Protection and promotion of the Diversity of Cultural Expressions*, Paris, UNESCO, 2005, article 8.

in any respect, interculturality can become a problem. Interculturality is often problematic, because racism and xenophobia are widespread, and locals and migrants often compete for limited resources or employment opportunities.

## 3.5. Minority and majority cultures

The term "minority culture" generally refers to the culture of marginalised or vulnerable groups of people who live in the shadow of majority populations with a different and dominant cultural ideology – the "majority culture". Other terms used for the majority culture and minority culture are "dominant culture" and "subculture" respectively. There can be linguistic, ethnic or religious minorities.[53] The criterion of minority is determined by subordinate or marginalised *status* rather than by numbers. Sometimes they can be more numerous than the "majority".[54] Generally in a majority culture, the language, religion, values, rules, rituals and social customs of the majority culture is norm for the society as a whole. The majority culture usually, but not always, controls the social institutions, such as, educational institutions, mass media, artistic expression, law, political processes, and businesses.

The defining characteristics of a minority culture are generally based on one or more observable characteristics such as ethnicity, race, nationality, religion, political influence, numerical weakness, etc. The minority cultural groups generally remain subordinate to the majority cultural group in political, financial, or social power. Critics argue

---

[53] Cf. Giuliana Gennai, *Lessico Interculturale*, p. 112. UNESCO has identified four different categories of minorities: indigenous peoples, territorial minorities with long cultural tradition, non-territorial minorities or nomads or people with no particular attachment to territory, and immigrants. Cf. http://unesdoc.unesco.org/images/0014/001478/147878e.pdf (1.5.2017).

[54] Cf. Charlotte Seymour-Smith, *Macmillan Dictionary of Anthropology*, p. 192.

that the minority cultures are often discriminated against by those who belong to the majority culture. In some countries, the minority cultural groups are protected under the law so that they can have certain rights to preserve and enhance their culture.

Today the use of the terms "majority culture" and "minority culture" is generally abandoned because they have been appropriated by majorities to stigmatise communities and spread prejudices against them through propaganda. It is also argued that cultural diversity should go beyond the "majority/minority" dichotomy and should speak of their complementarity.

## 4. Factors contributing to cultural pluralism

The world has always been culturally plural. However, the awareness of it has increased in recent decades due to many of factors. Obvious cultural differences exist between people, such as language, customs, social norms, gender relations, dress, food habits, religious practices, These differences also exists in variations in the way societies organise themselves, in their conception of morality, in their worldviews, and in the ways they interact with their environment. Consequently, many separate societies emerged around the globe which differed markedly in their culture from each other. There are many powerful forces responsible for the radical cultural pluralism of today. The following can be identified as the major ones:

### 4.1. Globalisation

Globalisation which is the process of increasing contact, interaction and collaboration between peoples and nations particularly has an effect on the world of culture. Globalisation is accelerating at an ever-greater pace and countries, peoples, cultures, religions and economies are drawing closer together and becoming more universal and intermingled. Globalisation has shown the plurality of cultures that characterise human society, and facilitates communication among various areas of the world, involving all facets of life. This is not just something theoretical or general: in fact, every individual is constantly affected by information and news that arrive from every part of the world. Today a person encounters, in everyday life, a variety of cultures, and thus experiences an increasing sense of belonging to what can be called the "global village".[55] A globalised world can leave certain human groups, especially minority cultures, exposed to loss of identity and impoverishment. Their values and structures can be weakened as they enter into a more globalised world.

## 4.2. Immigration and migratory movements

Today, the cultural composition of societies is growing even more complex through immigration increasing and migratory movements from one country to another and from rural to urban regions. Human migration is the process by which individuals or groups of people change their usual place of residence crossing administrative boundaries.[56] The movement is typically over long distances and from one country to another (international migration), and is done for the purpose of taking up permanent or semi-permanent residence. But there can also be migration within the country from rural to urban areas or from one cultural setting to another (internal migration). There is voluntary migration and forced migration due to war, political conflict, ethnic cleansing, religious persecution, slave trade, human trafficking, and other forms of human rights violation. In

---

[55] Cf. Congregation for Catholic Education, *Educating to intercultural dialogue in catholic schools*, no. 2.

[56] Cf. Ralf E. Ulrich, "Migration", in *Encyclopedia of Social Theory*, Austin Harrington, Barbara I. Marshall and Hans-Peter Müller (eds.), London, Routledge, 2006, p. 365.

forced migration, people are compelled by public authorities to leave their place of residence or they must escape in order to safeguard their lives. Refugees usually migrate on their own accord although they are generally under strong pressure or in danger while making this decision.[57] The role of information technology and quick means of transportation have also played a major role in migration.

It is importance to note that human beings have always migrated from prehistoric times and it is not a new reality of our time. *Before the Christian era,* two groups, the Semitics and the Indo-Europeans migrated. The Semitics from the Arabian Peninsula penetrated Mesopotamia and imposed themselves on the Sumerian population. The Indo-Europeans mixed themselves with the indigenous people of central and southern Europe giving birth to the great Greek civilisation. The *Medieval* period saw the migratory waves from North Europe and from the different regions of Asia looking for fertile land and conflict with the local population was created in the process. Later the Arabs penetrated the Iberian Peninsula and occupied it for many centuries. The Turks entered Europe and managed to reach up to Vienna. After the discovery of the Americas, there was migratory flows to the new lands, which increased in intensity in the beginning of the 18th century. It has been calculated that between 1820 and 1914 about 40 million Europeans journeyed to the United States. In Ireland the heavy taxes and the violence against the Catholics and Presbyterians by the government forced about 72% of the population to emigrate between 1851 and 1901. Towards the end of the 1800s, many Italians emigrated. It is said that about seven million Italians crossed the ocean and immigrated to other countries, especially to the countries of South America and to North America.[58] During the World

---

[57] Cf. Ibid.

[58] Cf. *Cultura e Identità in Gioco. Percorsi didattici interdisciplinari di educazione alla pace e al dialogo interculturale*, Maurizio Gusso, Lucia

War II many from Europe immigrated to other countries, especially Jews. After World War II the rapid economic development of Europe required more labourers and this favoured immigration from other countries. Colonisation also favoured immigration of people from the colonised countries to the country that colonised. Since 2014 Europe has been experiencing a massive immigration flow especially from the Middle East and Africa, and the continent is struggling to cope with it. Thus history tells us that the mobility of people is a recurrent phenomenon in human history. When people immigrate they take all of their cultural baggage with them.

Today, due to the strong process of migration, peoples and cultures of distant areas are able to relate with each other more than in the past. Migration has given rise to continuous changes in the social, political, religious, economic and cultural lives of people, both at the national and international levels. In many countries, the cultural composition of the cities has become very complex, and in schools and universities, there is a constant increase of students who belong to different ethnic, religious, cultural and linguistic groups.

Immigration and migratory movements can have *positive* and *negative* impacts on both the host country and the country of origin. If the immigrants are well educated in their country, and are made to feel welcome in the host country, they can contribute to the cultural diversity of that society and its economy. This in turn can lead to greater toleration, understanding and peaceful co-existence. But immigration can also have negative effects: it can mean a "brain drain" for the original country; immigrants can be exploited and abused, and their fundamental rights denied in the host country; immigrants can attract criminal elements and create cultural conflicts; immigration and migratory movements can lead to

---

Nadin e Michele Serra (a cura di), Bologna, Editrice Missionaria Italiana, 1995, pp. 59-60.

racist feelings and xenophobia among the local population, and political parties can exploit the sentiments of people for their political interests.

## 4.3. Mass media

Mass media[59] have played a major role in promoting cultural pluralism. The media bring information on societies and cultures, and promote increased interconnectedness among them. Media centres allow cultures to promote awareness, and provide knowledge and understanding of their stories and identities. Due to the unprecedented access to cultures through the media, a much wider audience than ever before has the opportunity to see, hear and experience the phenomenon of cultural pluralism. The advancement of media technology has dissolved international boundaries and opened cultures to a whole new arena. Thus the mass media are prominent amplifiers of cultural diversity in the world. In other words, the mass media have brought about a major alteration in human thought, both at the individual level and collective level, with regard to cultural pluralism and its complexity. Hence mass media can be considered as the most influential mediators, representatives and purveyors of values, beliefs and social practices of cultural entities.

Mass media have both *positive* and *negative* influences on cultural diversity. For example, they can empower cultures to preserve their identity. Instead of destroying some cultures, the media can assist them in revitalising and restoring them. But media can also misrepresent and stereotype certain cultures and spread prejudice against them through deliberate

---

[59] The term refers to the various vehicles used for sending information to a mass audience: radio, television, CATV, newspapers, magazines, books, discs, etc. Cf. R. Terry Ellmore, NTC's Mass Media Dictionary, Illinois, National Textbook Company, 1991, p. 351. The second half of the 20th century and the beginning of the 21st century saw a huge growth of media forms.

propaganda. It can work against cultural pluralism and its complexity and promote cultural homogenisation. The cultural nationalism, which is experienced in many parts of the world expresses a desperate attempt to preserve a cultural identity in the face of cultural homogenisation, and the real or presumed fear of the loss of one's culture.

## 5. Some negative attitudes towards cultural pluralism

In the face of cultural pluralism several negative attitudes are possible.[60] Some of the commonly noticed ones are the following:

### 5.1. Prejudice

Prejudice[61] usually refers to a negative, unjustified, incorrect preconceived *view* or *attitude* (not action) towards an individual based solely on his or her membership in a specific social group. It involves pre-judging individuals based on their affiliation to a particular cultural, racial, ethnic, religious or linguistic community. There can also be prejudice between cultures, which is called cultural bias. In this case,

---

[60] This does not mean that in all contexts of cultural pluralism only negative attitudes exist. In fact, there are admirable cases of positive attitudes towards cultural pluralism. In general, most people have a positive attitude towards it.

[61] The word "prejudice" means pre-judgement, implying that a prejudiced person is someone who has made up his mind about a certain topic before assessing the relevant information. Three other features associated with prejudiced belief are: a) prejudice typically refers to beliefs about social groups; it can also refer to judgement about individuals where an individual is evaluated on the basis of being a member of a particular social group; b) the belief or judgement is an unfavourable one, thus usually denotes a negative or hostile attitude against a group; c) a prejudiced belief is assumed to be erroneous or liable to lead the believer into error. A prejudice is not based on a realistic assessment of a social group nor is contact with the group likely to overturn the prejudices. Cf. Michael Billig, "Prejudice", in *The Social Science Encyclopedia*, Adam Kuper and Jessica Kuper (eds.), London, Routledge, 1985, p. 641.

prejudice is extended to a whole community. Cultures may demonstrate prejudices about others in a variety of ways including the stereotypes they apply to members of other groups. All cultures seem to make a distinction between "us" and "them" and "we" and "they", and they favour "us" and "we" over "them" and "they" for many reasons. Prejudice is often the result of ignorance and generalisation. It can lead to open aggression and hostility towards members of cultures not their own.

## 5.2. Discrimination

Discrimination[62] refers to the process of unjustly differentiating or the selection for unfavourable treatment of individuals or groups on the grounds of their, race, ethnicity, culture, language, gender, age, colour, socio-economic status, religion, nationality etc. Individual discrimination refers to the discrimination against one person by another. Cultural discrimination implies exclusion, restriction or hate that is directed at a person or a group on the basis of presumed or real differences in cultural values, beliefs and customs. It can take the form of discrimination against indigenous peoples, migrants, ethnic groups and religious minorities. Discrimination can be direct or indirect. Indirect discrimination is a discrete type of discrimination that involves a policy, rule or procedure that is applied to the disadvantage of certain groups of people. In discrimination what is at stake are human rights and fundamental freedoms. The reason for certain cultural groups forming a ghetto or living in isolation or in underprivileged urban areas as restricted and segregated, is often a result of discrimination.

---

[62] It comes from the Latin *discriminatio*, which means to perceive distinctions among phenomena or to be selective in one's judgement. Cf. Thomas F. Pettigrew and Marylee C. Taylor, "Discrimination", in *Encyclopaedia of Sociology*, Vol. 1, Edgar F. Borgatta (ed-), New York, Macmillan Publishing Company, 1992, p. 498.

## 5.3. Racism

Race denotes the belief that the human species is naturally grouped into distinct biological categories called "races". This belief is the basis of *biological racism*.[63] Racism is a doctrine or belief in racial superiority.[64] It involves the idea that one's own race is superior and has the right to dominate over others or that a particular racial group is inferior to the others. The result of racism is hatred or intolerance of another race or other races, prejudice, discrimination or antagonism. Nazism was a case of extreme racism.[65] Antisemitism[66] is widely considered to be a form of racism. Apartheid[67] is

---

[63] "Racism" is to be distinguished from "racialism". Racialism is a view that human beings are fundamentally grouped into races. Racism starts from the belief that human beings are grouped into races and then *adds* the belief that these races are of differential intrinsic *worth*. Cf. Brian Alleyne, "'Race' and Racism", in *Encyclopedia of Social Theory*, Austin Harrington, Barbara I. Marshall and Hans-Peter Müller, London, Routledge, 2006, p. 490.

[64] Cf. Charlotte Seymour-Smith, *Macmillan Dictionary of Anthropology*, p. 238. A racist is one who believes in the superiority or inferiority of individuals of a specific "race" and gives it a biological explanation. Cf. Anna Maria Fantauzzi, "Razzismo biologico, razzismo differenzialista?" p. 150.

[65] Cf. Brian Alleyne, "'Race' and Racism", p. 491.

[66] Antisemitism is a term (derived from *Semites* = descendants of the biblical Shem, and *anti* = against) used since the close of the 19th century to designate the organised movement or the manifestations of hatred against the Jews. The "theory" of modern anti-Semitism was ultimately based on the distinction between the Aryan and Semitic language groups and the Aryan and Semitic "races". The Aryans were depicted as the elite of humanity and the others represented by the Jews were regarded as its antithesis. The term "anti-Semitism" was coined by the German journalist Wilhelm Marr in 1879 to designate anti-Jewish movement, and it achieved great popularity. Cf. *The New Standard Jewish Encyclopaedia*, Cecil Roth and Geoffrey Wigoder (eds.), Jerusalem, Massada Press, 5th edition, 1977, pp. 120-121.

[67] "Apartheid" is an Afrikaans (one of the official languages of South Africa) word meaning "the state of being apart". The suffix *heid* means "state or condition" and *apart* means "separated". Hence Apartheid means "apartness" or "separation" or "segregation" in all spheres of life, private

another example of racism. The Hindu caste system[68] can also be considered as a species of racism because it involves the belief that the people of the upper castes are superior to those of the lower castes, and it is birth that determines the caste.

Besides biological racism, today people also speak of *culture racism* (known also as "cultural racism").[69] It refers to cultures instead of the ancestry of different peoples and thus differs from biological racism. It is the notion that cultures are absolute, unchangeable and define an individual's characteristics. It exists when there is a widespread acceptance of stereotypes concerning different ethnic or racial or cultural groups. Cultural racism includes a belief that one's own ethnic group's cultural heritage is superior to that of

---

and public. It was a system used in South Africa to segregate whites from non-whites (i.e., the native black population and the Asiatic minorities). It involves the belief in white racial purity and supremacy. The practice has its roots in the white master/slave relationships of the seventeenth-century colonialism. Cf. Giuliana Gennai, *Lessico Interculturale*, p. 22; Ellis Cashmore, "Apartheid", in *Dictionary of Race and Ethnic Relations*, E. Ellis Cashmore, Michael Banton, *et al*, (eds.), London, Routledge, 1988, p. 18.

[68] "Caste" is derived from the Portuguese word *castas*. It was used by the Western observers to identify the social units among the Indian Hindus. The ancient Indian society since about 1000 B.C was divided into four *varnas* (literally it means "colour" but signifies "class"): the *Brahmanas* or priests, the *Kshatriyas* or worriers, the *Vaisyas* or the farmers, traders and producers of wealth, and the *Sudras* or the people who served these three higher groups. Eventually outside these four groups came to be considered the untouchables constituting a fifth category known as *Panchamas* or *Ati-Sudras* or *Chandalas*. Cf. Sekhar Bandyopadhyay, "Caste", in *Encyclopedia of Social Theory*, Austin Harrington, Barbara I. Marshall and Hans-Peter Müller, London, Routledge, 2006, p. 48.

[69] "Cultural racism" is one of the several terms which scholars have coined to describe and explain new racial ideologies and practices that have emerged since World War II. This term was first used in the beginning of the 1980s. In England and the United States the terms "new racism" (coined by the sociologist Martin Barker) and "ethnicisation" are also used to describe the same phenomenon. During the 1980s and the 1990s, cultural racism came to replace the previously generally accepted forms of biological racism.

other ethnic groups. Thus cultural differences legitimize exclusion and discrimination based on racial notions and the ranking of cultures as higher and lower in relation to each other.

Some scholars speak of "differentialist racism" (*razzismo differenzialista*) as a masked form of racism in our contemporary society. It is an application of the logic of separation, exclusion and difference on the basis of culture, religion, etc., which encourages people to remain "outside" without integration. They have a fear of mixing with other human groups and are obsessed with the fear of losing their purity of lineage identity. This opens the way for an indifferent separation where each one organizes their own way of transmitting their values and ensures that there is no contact, hybridisation and crossbreeding.[70]

Many social and cultural anthropologists of the twentieth century insisted that "race" was a social and not a natural category. They moved away from biologically based notions of differences between human populations. They argued that human groups were different because culture manifested itself in different ways. Besides this critical observation, the life sciences, and even simple logic deny the existence of "races" as clearly defined groups of people. Yet the idea that "race" is somehow natural and even immutable retains much currency.[71]

## 5.4. Xenophobia

Xenophobia[72] is an attitude of fear, contempt and hostility

---

[70] Cf. Anna Maria Fantauzzi, "Razzismo biologico, razzismo differenzialista?", pp. 162-163.

[71] Cf. Brian Alleyne, "'Race' and Racism", pp. 491-492.

[72] The term is coined from two Greek words *xenos* (foreigner) and *fobos* (fear). Cf. Giuliana Gennai, *Lessico Interculturale*, p. 150. The Oxford English Dictionary describes "xenophobia" as a deep antipathy for foreigners. Cf. *The Oxford English Dictionary*, Vol. 20, Oxford, Clarendon

directed against non-natives in a given population. It implies a behaviour based on the idea that the other is foreign to or originates from outside one's community or nation. The term is strictly related to racism, ethnocentrism and nationalism.[73] Often xenophobia is directed against recent immigrants, but it may be directed also against a group, which has been present for centuries or became part of a society through conquest and territorial expansion. All cultures can be subject to xenophobia. Xenophobia can manifest itself in many ways involving relations and perceptions of an "in-group" towards an "out-group," including a fear of losing one's identity and the desire to eliminate its presence to secure a presumed purity. Xenophobic behaviour is based on existing racist, ethnic, religious, cultural or national prejudices. This form of xenophobia can elicit or facilitate hostile and violent reactions such as mass expulsion of immigrants, pogroms or in other cases, genocide. Entirely xenophobic societies tend not to be open to interactions from anything "outside" themselves, resulting in isolationism that can further increase xenophobia. Hate speech and hate crimes are typical manifestations of xenophobia.

Another form of xenophobia is *cultural*, and the objects of the phobia are cultural elements, which are considered foreign. All cultures are subject to external influences, but cultural xenophobia is often narrowly directed, for instance, at foreign loan words in a national language or certain customs and practices that seem to come from outside a culture. Xenophobia can also be exhibited in the form of an uncritical exaltation of one's own culture in which it is ascribed an unreal, stereotyped and exotic quality, greatness

Press, 2nd edition, 1989, p. 674. The Webster's English Dictionary states that xenophobia is fear and hatred of strangers or foreigners or of anything that is strange or foreign. Cf. *Webster's Third New International Dictionary of the English Language Unabridged,* Vol. 3., Chicago, Encyclopedia Britannica, 1986, p. 2644.

[73] Cf. Giuliana Gennai, *Lessico Interculturale*, p. 150.

and purity and rejection of everything different from it. This kind of attitude can result in political campaigns for cultural or linguistic purification. Cultural nationalisms foster this form of xenophobia.

## 5.5. Ethnocentrism

Another danger to cultural pluralism is ethnocentrism. Ethnocentrism refers to the habit or tendency to judge or interpret other cultures according to the criterion of one's own culture.[74] This implies that that one's ethnic group is at the centre of everything and all others are classified and evaluated in relation to it.[75] It is said that there are three levels of ethnocentrism: a positive one, a negative one, and an extreme negative one. The *positive* definition defines ethnocentrism as the point of view that one's own way of life is to be preferred to all others. There is nothing wrong with such feelings for it characterises the way most individuals feel about their own cultures, whether or not they verbalise their feeling.[76] It is ethnocentrism that gives people their sense of belonging to a particular people, group identity, and place in history – all of which are valuable traits to possess. Ethnocentrism becomes *negative* when one's own group becomes the centre of everything, and all others are measured and rated with reference to it. It reaches its *extreme negative* form when a more powerful group not only imposes its rules and norms on others, but also actively depreciates the things

---

[74] Cf. Charlotte Seymour-Smith, *Macmillan Dictionary of Anthropology*, p. 97.

[75] Cf. Giuliana Gennai, *Lessico Interculturale*, p. 57. Ethnocentrism makes the distinction between "in-group" and "out-group". In "primitive" society the attitude towards the "in-group" was marked by peace and collaboration, and hostility and aggression towards the "out-group" Cf. A. M. Boileau, "Etnocentrismo", in *Nuovo Dizionario di Sociologia*, Franco Demarchi, Aldo Ellena e Bernardo Cattarinussi (a cura di), Milano, Edizioni Paoline, 1987, p. 804.

[76] Cf. Melville J. Herskovits, *Man and His Works*, p. 68.

they hold to be of value.

Ethnocentrism has a negative connotation. It implies a cultural narrow-mindedness that does not lend itself to overcoming cultural gaps or learning how to interact and dialogue with people from different cultures and live in peace with them. Extreme negative ethnocentrism is a characteristic of cultural nationalism and shows itself to be essentially an undemocratic political attitude. Antisemitism, apartheid, ethnic cleansing and genocide are all examples of extreme negative ethnocentrism.

## 5.6. Ghettoization

The people of particular groups who share common ethnic and cultural characteristics in specific sectors of the city often take the form of a segregated area that is described as a ghetto. A ghetto has a high degree of homogeneity and all residents share similar backgrounds, beliefs, etc. Usually their living conditions are poor in relation to the rest of the city's population.[77] Often ghettoization takes place because of social, cultural, religious, legal, or economic pressure or discrimination or denial of human rights. As a result, people live as sidelined minority groups and are kept out of the mainstream either physically or culturally. They live in exclusion, marginalisation, and as victims of discrimination and control by the majority groups.

## 5.7. Denial of human rights

Human rights are moral principles or norms that describe certain standards of human behaviour, and are regularly protected as legal rights in municipal and international law. They are commonly understood as inalienable fundamental

---

[77] Cf. Barry Troyna, "Ghetto", in *Dictionary of Race and Ethnic Relations*, E. Ellis Cashmore, Michael Banton, *et al*, (eds.), London, Routledge, 1988, p. 118.

rights to which a person is inherently entitled simply because she or he is a human being, and which are inherent in all human beings regardless of their nation, language, religion, gender, culture, colour, ethnic origin or any other status. They are applicable everywhere and at every time in the sense of being universal, and they are egalitarian in the sense of being the same for everyone. In principle, all are equally entitled to human rights without discrimination because they have their foundation in human nature. However, individuals and groups can be denied basic human rights because of their ethnic origin, religion, nationality, language and cultural values and because they are cultural minorities and vulnerable groups. This seriously violates fundamental human rights. The UNESCO resolution of 2001 emphatically stated that none should invoke cultural diversity to deny people their human rights:

> The defence of cultural diversity is an ethical imperative, inseparable from respect for human dignity. It implies a commitment to human rights and fundamental freedoms, in particular the rights of persons belonging to minorities and those of indigenous peoples. No one may invoke cultural diversity to infringe upon human rights guaranteed by international law, nor to limit their scope.[78]

## 5.8. Denial of cultural rights

Cultural rights are human rights that aim at assuring the enjoyment of culture and its components in conditions of equality, human dignity and non-discrimination. As stated above, in the context of cultural pluralism human rights mean that no one may invoke cultural diversity to infringe upon human rights guaranteed by international law nor limit their

---

[78] *Records of the General Conference*, 31st Session, Paris 15 October to 3 November 2001, Vol. 1, *Resolutions*, Paris, UNESCO, 2002. Annex 1, p. 63.

scope. The emphasis is on acknowledgment, understanding and tolerance of other cultures on the basis of a binding global ethic founded on universal values and mutual respect across cultural boundaries. The cultural rights movement has provoked attention to protect the rights of groups of people or their culture. The UNESCO resolution of 2001 on cultural diversity affirmed the following: "Cultural rights are an integral part of human rights, which are universal, indivisible and interdependent. The flourishing of creative diversity requires the full implementation of cultural rights."[79]

Thus the link between cultural diversity and human rights was clearly established by the Universal Declaration on Cultural Diversity, adopted by the Member States of UNESCO in 2001.[80] In the context of cultural pluralism certain persons and groups can be denied fundamental rights, such as the right to life, equality before the law, freedom of speech, religious liberty, freedom of conscience, right to private property, etc. In such situations often it is a cultural minority that suffers at the hands of powerful cultural majority.

## 5.9. Attempt to impose monoculturalism

Monoculturalism consists in actively preserving a national culture through the exclusion of external influences. It encourages a normative cultural unity or cultural homogeneity. It possesses negative attributes due to its encouragement of ethnocentrism, cultural absolutism, naïve realism, lack of respect for and suppression of cultures different from one's own. Its greatest advantage is the sense of identity as a nation and its political attraction. Usually a monocultural society exists due to racial homogeneity, nationalistic tendencies, religious fundamentalism,

---

[79] Ibid.

[80] For details see Ibid., Annex 1 and 2, pp. 62-64.

geographic isolation, or political isolation (sometimes, but not always, under a totalitarian regime). Different methods are used to impose a monoculture on a population, such as, imposition of certain homogenous laws, homogenous language, mobilisation of education, imposing a majority religion on minority groups, changing a democratic secular constitution of a nation to favour a specific religion or culture or ideology. Monoculturalism is cultural conservatism and is generally held in disdain. Fear of diversity is at the basis of attempt to impose monoculture.

## 5.10. Cultural Conflicts

In culturally pluralistic societies lack of cultural understanding and cultural integration can lead to conflicts. Conflict can be defined as a struggle over power, scarce resources or values in which conflicting parties seek to realise their interests.[81] It is a situation in which different parties holding incompatible views take action against each other. Some nations and cultures refuse to be multi-ethnic and multi-cultural. Cultural conflicts can occur when cultural diversity is seen as a threat to social cohesion and national unity. It can occur when different cultural values, beliefs and traditions clash and can take direct or indirect forms. It will be manifested in the attitudes of political organisations, groups, political policies, media (television, radio, internet, etc.), educational programmes and even in the ordinary attitudes and conversations of people. Sometimes it can take aggressive forms like protests, demonstrations, debates in the media and in the parliament, and other times it takes subtle forms. Cultural conflicts can lead even to violence and crime.

There are many reasons for cultural conflicts. Some of them can be identified as the following:

---

[81] Cf. Jürgen Mackert, "Conflict", in *Encyclopedia of Social Theory*, Austin Harrington, Barbara I. Marshall and Hans-Peter Müller, London, Routledge, 2006, pp. 90-91.

*Mutual ignorance* is one of the major causes of cultural conflict. Different countries or cultures have different lifestyles and practices due to their different levels of development. Differences in cultural practices, religious beliefs, value systems, customs, traditions, habits, language etc., can cause mutual ignorance. The theory of "Clash of Ignorance"[82] highlights cultural ignorance as the primary source of tension, hostility and conflict between cultures.

Often *ethnicity and religious affiliation* are concepts around which discussion and controversy arise, generating emotions and feelings of extreme intensity. All people belong to such a community. By default, there is pressure on people and institutions to be subjective. When an ethnic or religious group faces discrimination, marginalisation, denied fundamental human rights, or is given a low-status as minorities, treated as peripheral societies, and made victims of inequitable distribution of resources, cultural conflict can occur.

*The absence of a clear distinction between religion, politics and society* can lead to cultural conflict. The countries where Islam dominates have a cultural world of their own, although there are differences between the Arab countries and the other countries of Africa and Asia. Islam is not just a religion in the classic sense of the word: it is also essentially a society with its own legislation and traditions, and the whole forms a vast community or *umma*, with its own culture and plan for civilisation.[83] Similar problem exists,

---

[82] "The Clash of Ignorance" refers to a theory developed by Columbia University professor Edward Said's essay titled "The Clash of Ignorance" first appeared in the 22 October 2001 edition of *The Nation*, published shortly after the 11 September 2001 attacks. Cf. https://www.scribd.com/document/190875354/Said-Edward-W-The-Clash-of-Ignorance-The-Nation-Article-samuel-huntingtoncivilizations-pdf (29.12.2017)

[83] Cf. Pontifical Council for Culture, *Towards a Pastoral Approach to Culture,* no. 22.

perhaps in lesser degrees, in certain countries where Hinduism and Buddhism are the religion of the majority, and where they try to impose their religion and culture on others who belong to a different religion or culture, using political power and the pressure of social conformism.

The *contrast between secularised cultures and religious cultures can led to cultural conflict.* Secularised cultures have a profound influence in various parts of the world. In a secularised society religion loses much of its social, cultural and institutional significance. As a result the role of religion in modern societies becomes restricted. When secularisation transforms itself into secularism there is a serious cultural and spiritual crisis.[84] When a secularised culture encounters a deeply religious culture or *vice versa*, tensions can arise, and it can lead to cultural conflict. This is especially true when religious fundamentalism and secularised ideologies meet.

It would be wrong to hold that ethnic and cultural differences are the cause of all the conflicts that disturb the world. In truth, these conflicts have *political, economic, ethnic, religious and territorial causes* and are certainly not exclusively, or primarily, cultural conflicts. However, cultural, historical and symbolic elements are used to stir people up, to the point of encouraging violence rooted in elements of economic competition, social contrasts and political absolutism.[85]

## 6. Approaches to cultural pluralism

In the context of cultural pluralism one can adopt at least three approaches: the relativistic approach, the assimilation approach or the intercultural approach. Each has its own advantages and disadvantages. Below is a brief explanation of

---

[84] Cf. Ibid., no. 23.
[85] Cf. Congregation for Catholic Education, *Educating to intercultural dialogue in catholic schools*, no. 5.

these three approaches:

## 6.1. Relativistic approach

The relativistic approach is based on the theory of cultural relativism. Cultural relativism raises a problem in that it tends to view reality exclusively from its own narrow perspective. It maintains that each culture or ethnic group is to be evaluated on the basis of its own values, institutions and norms of behaviour and not on the basis of those of another culture or ethnic group. In other words, it affirms a profound incompatibility between cultures, a kind of autonomy of ethical models and self-validation of cultural values and promotes the idea that no culture can claim superiority over another[86] with regard to values, beliefs, customs, habits, traditions, morality, law, forms of governance, etc. This means that, all cultural beliefs are equally valid, and truth itself is relative depending on the cultural environment. Hence each culture must be examined in terms of its own structure and norms, instead of being rated by the standards of some other civilisation exalted as absolute.

The Vatican Congregation for Catholic Education affirms that being aware of the relative nature of cultures and opting for relativism are two totally different things. To recognise that reality is historical and changeable does not necessarily lead to a relativistic approach. Relativism, on the other hand, respects differences, but also separates them out into autonomous spheres, considering them as isolated and impermeable and making dialogue impossible. Relativistic "neutrality" endorses the absolute nature of every culture within its own sphere, and impedes the use of meta-cultural critical judgement, which would otherwise allow for universal interpretations. The relativistic model is founded on the value of tolerance, but limits itself to accepting the other

---

[86] Cf. Hervé Carrier, *Dizionario della Cultura*, p. 328.

person, excluding the possibility of dialogue and recognition of each other in mutual transformation. Such an idea of tolerance, in fact, leads to a substantially passive meaning of relationship with whoever has a different culture. It does not demand that one take an interest in the needs and sufferings of others, nor that their reasons may be heard; there is no self-comparison with their values, and even less sense of developing love for them.[87]

The relativistic approach is at the basis of the political and social model of multiculturalism. This model offers no adequate solutions for co-existence and fails to encourage true intercultural dialogue. "[…] one may observe a *cultural eclecticism* that is often assumed uncritically: cultures are simply placed alongside one another and viewed as substantially equivalent and interchangeable. This easily yields to a relativism that does not serve true intercultural dialogue; on the social plane, cultural relativism has the effect that cultural groups coexist side by side, but remain separate, with no authentic dialogue and therefore with no true integration."[88] Another problem with multiculturalism is that it fosters communal segregation and mutual incomprehension and contributes to the undermining of the rights of individuals and of minority communities.

Nevertheless, the relativistic approach is an attitude that is of fundamental *methodological importance* because it calls attention to the local context in understanding the meaning of particular human beliefs and activities. But people can also misinterpret the relativistic approach to mean that all cultures are both separate and equal and that all value systems, however different, are equally valid. Here what is at stake is objective truth and universal norms and values. It implies the

---

[87] Cf. Congregation for Catholic Education, *Educating to intercultural dialogue in catholic schools*, no. 22.

[88] Benedict XVI, Encyclical Letter *Caritas in Veritate* (29 June 2009), in *Acta Apostolicae Sedis,* 101 (2009), no. 26.

exaltation of the subjective, and truth is considered as relative. The sense of openness to other cultures, cultural comparison, cultural dialogue and learning from others cannot be conceived as they are not needed because each culture is absolute and self-sufficient in its own right. Hervé Carrier notes that the great danger of cultural pluralism is that it promotes moral relativism so that the concepts of good and bad have no universal value but vary according to time and society.[89]

Cultural relativism promotes a misguided understanding of pluralism and tolerance. It exaggerates cultural differences and provides no common meeting ground between cultures and advocates a sort of ethnocentrism. Cultural relativism may *appear* to uphold tolerance of cultural differences, yet it may support intolerance because cultural values of a group may demand intolerance. Because of these reasons the relativistic approach to cultures cannot be endorsed.

## 6.2. Assimilative approach

Cultural assimilation[90] (known also as "cultural integration or incorporation") is an acculturation process in which the subordinate or small groups are absorbed into the larger or dominant one and becomes indistinguishable from it in cultural terms.[91] The term is used to refer to both individuals and groups, and in the latter case it can refer to either immigrant diasporas or native residents that come to be culturally dominated by another society. Assimilation may involve either a quick or gradual change depending on

---

[89] Cf. Hervé Carrier, *Dizionario della Cultura*, p. 328.

[90] Assimilation means becoming similar. In sociology it is taken to mean a kind of ethnic change in which people become similar, and contrasted with differentiation. Cf. Michael Banton, "Assimilation", in *Dictionary of Race and Ethnic Relations*, E. Ellis Cashmore, Michael Banton, *et al*, (eds.), London, Routledge, 1988, pp. 25-26.

[91] Cf. Charlotte Seymour-Smith, *Macmillan Dictionary of Anthropology*, p. 18.

circumstances of the group. Full assimilation occurs when new members of a society become indistinguishable from members of the other group.

Immigrant assimilation is a complex process in which immigrants not only fully integrate themselves into a new country but also lose aspects, perhaps also their entire cultural heritage. Some minorities consciously adopt practices designed to resist the pressures towards cultural assimilation. In other circumstances members of the majority may impede assimilation by withholding social acceptance.[92] The members of the group and those of the dominant society often dispute whether or not it is desirable for an immigrant group to assimilate.

The Vatican Congregation for Catholic Education affirms that what is called the assimilation approach is certainly *not satisfying*. Rather than indifference towards the other culture, this approach is characterised by the demand for the other person to adapt. An example would be when, in a country with mass immigration, the presence of the foreigner is accepted only on the condition that he or she renounces his or her identity and cultural roots so as to embrace those of the receiving country. In educational models based on assimilation, the other person must abandon his or her cultural references, to take on those of another group or of the receiving country. Exchange is reduced to the mere insertion of minority cultures in the majority one, with little or no attention to the other person's culture of origin.[93]

More generally, the assimilation approach is advanced by a culture with universal pretensions, which seeks to impose its own cultural values by means of its economic, commercial, military and cultural influence. Here the danger is that of *cultural levelling* and indiscriminate acceptance of

---

[92] Cf. Michael Banton, "Assimilation", p. 26.

[93] Cf. Congregation for Catholic Education, *Educating to intercultural dialogue in catholic schools*, no. 24.

types of conduct and life-styles.[94]

Assimilative approach implies domination, and often it is accomplished through "violence" and "force", which can be physical, moral or psychological. A cultural group can also spontaneously adopt a different culture due to its political relevance, or its perceived superiority or for some specific advantage. Generally, it is a culture of subordinate status that succumbs to assimilation. Nevertheless, assimilation is not an appropriate way to deal with cultural diversity because *it promotes a homogenous model of society or monoculture and negates the cultural identity of the other*.

The teaching of the Catholic Church is clearly against cultural assimilation. For example, Pope John Paul II said on 8 February 1993 in Uganda while addressing the Diplomatic Corps that in Africa's future there should be no room for schemes, which seek to fabricate national unity by forcing minorities to assimilate the culture or religion of the majority. False unity only leads to tragedy. In this regard religious liberty must be respected everywhere.[95] On 10 February 1993 he said in Khartoum, Sudan: "All that the Church asks for is the freedom to pursue her religious and humanitarian mission. This freedom is her right, for it is everyone's duty, the duty of individuals and of the State, to respect the conscience of every human being".[96] Thus cultural minorities within a country have the right to exist, with their own language, culture and traditions, irrespective of racial, ethnic, cultural or national origin or religious belief, and the State is morally obliged to leave room for their identity and self-expression.[97]

---

[94] Cf. Benedict XVI, *Caritas in Veritate*, no. 26.

[95] Cf. *Insegnamenti di Giovanni Paolo II*, Vol. XVI, parte 1, Citta del Vaticano, Libraria Editrice Vaticana, 1995, p. 365.

[96] Ibid., p. 397.

[97] Cf. Ibid., p. 405.

## 6.3. Intercultural approach

An alternative to the relativistic approach and the assimilation approaches is the intercultural approach. This is positively promoted by the Catholic Church and the magisterium of the Popes, especially since Vatican Council II. The intercultural approach aims to establish a dialogue and co-operation between co-existing cultures and manifests respect for cultural diversity. Today the possibilities of interaction between cultures have increased significantly, giving rise to new openings for intercultural dialogue: a dialogue that, if it is to be effective, has to set out from a deep-seated knowledge of the specific identity of the various dialogue partners. From this point of view, diversity ceases to be seen as a problem. Instead, a community characterised by pluralism is seen as a resource, a chance for opening up the whole system to all differences of origin, relationships between men and women, social status and educational history.[98] It is argued that without biodiversity, species can atrophy. Similarly, in human terms, a culture cannot develop without diversity. The history of any cultural group shows that it is through dealing with the external and the different that they have evolved.[99]

The intercultural approach is based on a dynamic idea of culture, which is neither closed in on itself nor celebrates diversity with stereotypes. Intercultural strategies function when they avoid separating individuals into autonomous and impermeable cultural spheres; instead, they should promote encounter, dialogue and mutual transformation, so as to allow people to co-exist and deal with possible conflict. Thus the goal is to construct a new intercultural approach, which aims

---

[98] Cf. Congregation for Catholic Education, *Educating to intercultural dialogue in catholic schools*, no. 27.

[99] Cf. Phil Wood and Charles Landry, *The Intercultural City. Planning for Diversity Advantage*, London, Earthscan, 2008, p. 6.

at realizing an integration of cultures in mutual recognition.[100]

Thus the intercultural approach affirms the cultural identity of each one and their autonomy. It promotes mutual appreciation and respect for cultures. The encounter of cultures leads to discovery of common elements in cultures and mutual enrichment. There is neither the domination over a minority culture by a majority culture, nor the danger of assimilation of a subculture by a dominant one. No single culture claims to be absolute or superior to others or imposes its cultural values on others. There is room for intercultural criticism and acceptance of meta-cultural universal principles and norms. Intercultural approach promotes toleration and reduces cultural conflicts. Hence today this is the preferred approach to cultural pluralism.

## Conclusion

As we have seen, culture is a complex concept with many characteristics, and consequently it is not easy to define. Yet there exist numerous definitions. Today the world is dominated by cultural pluralism. While this phenomenon has many advantages, it is also capable of creating cultural conflicts, which can seriously challenge the peaceful co-existence of peoples and peace in the world. Cultural integration is important in today's world, but the model suggested for it is neither the relativistic approach nor the assimilation approach but the intercultural approach which alone can genuinely affirm cultural identity and pave way for authentic and meaningful intercultural interaction, dialogue and co-operation in order to build a more humane and peaceful world.

---

[100] Cf. Congregation for Catholic Education, *Educating to intercultural dialogue in catholic schools*, no. 28.

**Chapter 2**

# INTERCULTURAL DIALOGUE
## Meaning, Aims, Conditions and Forms

## Introduction

The world is rapidly changing and becoming more and more pluralistic culturally, religiously, linguistically, politically, and ideologically. The phenomena of globalisation, mass migration, the modern means of transport and impact of mass media are accelerating this process. As a consequence, an increasing number of people are facing the challenge of encountering cultural diversity. Cultural pluralism brings with it new social, economic, religious, political, ideological and ethical problems. It often leads to an attitudes of suspicion, fear and rejection in people, and it generates prejudice, discrimination, intolerance, inequality, stereotyping, racism, xenophobia, ghettoization and cultural conflicts, which threaten to damage social fabric, national unity and world peace. But if one has good will and is open-minded, cultural pluralism can be accepted and lived as 'new opportunities' for mutual enrichment. It is in this context that dialogue between cultures becomes imperative, and the only civilised way of promoting cultural integration in order to prevent ethnic, religious, linguistic cultural divides and cultural conflicts. The objective of this form of dialogue is to enable peoples of different cultures to live together in peace and harmony and construct a world where human dignity, human rights and democratic principles are respected, and cultural pluralism is seen not as a threat but as a resource, an opportunity and strength.

## 1. Meaning and nature of intercultural dialogue

Intercultural dialogue means interaction between different cultures. The concept implies more than a mere conversation between two individuals or groups of people. It refers to the whole gamut of interactive communication and collaborative initiatives for common good between persons, groups or larger communities. It can involve a wide range of actors such as individuals and groups, local organisations and international agencies, political leaders and governments, private associations and civil administrative bodies, religious leaders and followers of secular ideologies.

There are different understandings of intercultural dialogue, but there is no universally accepted definition. In 2008, the Council of Europe within the context of its "White Paper on Intercultural Dialogue" made an attempt to define it. It stated: "*Intercultural dialogue* is understood as an open and respectful exchange of views between individuals, groups with different ethnic, cultural, religious and linguistic backgrounds and heritage on the basis of mutual understanding and respect."[101] Another definition is: "intercultural dialogue is the interactive communication between cultures which aims at acquiring a deeper understanding of diverse cultural perspectives and practices for the management of cultural diversity in a democratic way and for promoting integration in a culturally pluralistic society."[102]

Intercultural dialogue includes all beneficial and constructive exchange between cultures, individuals and groups in order to arrive at mutual acceptance, understanding and reciprocal enrichment. It fosters equality, human dignity and a sense of common purpose and challenges the self-segregation tendencies within cultures and promotes communication between them. In this sense, it goes beyond mere tolerance of other cultures. Dialogue of cultures is a major means for managing diversity and strengthening democracy. It is a powerful instrument to prevent cultures from being marginalised and cultural conflicts due to failure in cultural integration.

Anyone with good will and the desire to enhance common good can participate in intercultural dialogue. It can be practiced worldwide between peoples, societies, nations, institutions and civilisations. It excludes none. Just as culture is a complex concept, intercultural dialogue is also complex and embraces every sphere of human activity. It can take up any matter for dialogue, which is related to the social and cultural life of people: political, economic, moral, religious, aesthetic, scientific, technological, national and international issues. Intercultural dialogue is not considered to be an immediate solution to problems but rather a measure that will benefit peace, reconciliation, integration, national and

---

[101] *White Paper on Intercultural Dialogue "Living Together as equals in dignity"*, Strasbourg, Council of Europe Ministers of Foreign Affairs, 2008, p. 10. (Italics in the original)

[102] This definition is of the present author.

international stability in the long term, even with respect to the threat of terrorism and war.

Today intercultural dialogue has become the dominant paradigm for the "cultural policy" of most governments and many leading regional, national and international organisations. It is the foundation for the functioning of many educational institutions in multicultural societies. Renowned scholars and outstanding institutions are now exploring the social, anthropological, historical, philosophical, theological and educational dimensions of intercultural dialogue. The Catholic Church and the magisterium of the Popes since Vatican Council II have underscored the importance of intercultural dialogue and are in the vanguard of promoting it.

## 2. Necessity of intercultural dialogue

Intercultural dialogue is assumed to be a pre-requisite for social cohesion and peace at national and international levels.[103] The old approaches to the management of cultural diversity are no longer adequate. The relativistic and assimilation approaches are being rejected, and the need for achieving inclusive societies requires a new approach based on intercultural dialogue.

Intercultural dialogue is born not out of a static idea of culture, but of its fundamental openness to the higher values common to all. The phenomenon of the reciprocal penetration of cultures illustrates this openness. Therefore, cultural pluralism cannot be interpreted as the juxtaposition of a closed universe but as participation in unison of realities all

---

[103] It may be recalled that the General Assembly of the United Nations proclaimed the year 2001 as the "United Nations Year of Dialogue among Civilizations". It invited governments, educational, social and cultural organizations of the world to plan and implement appropriate cultural, educational and social programmes to promote the concept of dialogue among civilizations. It also published a book entitled *Crossing the Divide. Dialogue among civilizations*, New Jersey, Seton Hall University, 2001.

directed toward the universal values. Hence it is the potential universality of every culture that establishes the foundation for intercultural dialogue.[104] Consequently, dialogue between cultures emerges as an intrinsic demand of human nature itself, as well as of culture based on the recognition that there are values, which are common to all cultures because they are rooted in the nature of the human person. Dialogue is necessary to foster people's awareness of these shared values, in order to nurture that intrinsically universal cultural "soil" which makes for fruitful and constructive dialogue.[105] The openness to higher values common to the entire human race based on universal values like truth, justice, peace, rule of law, dignity of the human person, openness to the transcendent, freedom of conscience and of religion, implies an idea of culture as being a contribution to a broader awareness of humanity. This is opposed to the tendency existing in the history of cultures, to build particular little worlds that are closed and introverted.[106] Thus by nature co-existence of different cultures entails dialogue, not confrontation.

To uphold the primacy of the human person is another reason for intercultural dialogue. Dialogue between cultures can help to defend fundamental human rights. The Universal Declaration of Human Rights in 1948 in thirty articles affirmed the importance of the human person. The second generation of human rights in 1966 did the same. In the

---

[104] Cf. International Theological Commission, "Faith and Inculturation", in *Texts and Documents 1986-2007*, Vol. II, Michael Sharkey and Thomas Weinandy (eds.), San Francisco, Ignatius Press, 2009, no. 7, p. 5.

[105] Cf. John Paul II, "*Dialogo tra le culture per una civiltà dell'amore e della pace*", Messaggio per la celebrazione della Giornata mondiale della pace (8 dicembre 2000), In *Insegnamenti di Giovanni Paolo II*, Vol. XXIII, parte 2, Città del Vaticano, Libraria Editrice Vaticana, 2002, nos. 10, 16.

[106] Cf. Congregation for Catholic Education, *Educating to intercultural dialogue in catholic schools: living in harmony for a civilization of love*, Città del Vaticano, Libreria Editrice Vaticana, 2013, no. 33.

Vienna convention of 1993, it was signed by 171 States.[107]

The practice of intercultural dialogue at the global level is required to help peoples and nations turn away from the logic of might, war, force, hegemony, discrimination, oppression and injustice. Dialogue is needed to live together as equals in a culturally pluralistic world and to avoid the "clash of civilisations", and for achieving international security. Because of these reasons, today, States, civil societies, political parties, international organisations and world religions understand the fundamental need for intercultural dialogue more and more.

Intercultural dialogue can prevent ethnic, religious, linguistic and cultural divides and help people move forward together to deal with different identities constructively and democratically on the basis of shared universal values.[108] The risks of non-dialogue can easily lead to a stereotyped perception of the other, build up a climate of mutual suspicion, tension and anxiety, use minorities as scapegoats and foster intolerance and discrimination, and in some cases even exploitation, extremism and terrorism.[109] The absence of dialogue deprives everyone of its benefit of new cultural openings necessary for personal and social development in a globalised world.[110]

## 3. Conditions for intercultural dialogue

In order that interreligious dialogue may be fruitful, certain conditions will have to be fulfilled from the very outset. There is a difference between the "culture of dialogue" and the and the "dialogue among cultures". The first important condition for intercultural dialogue is

---

[107] Cf. *Human Rights in the Intercultural Dialogue*, Cologne, Konrad Adenauer Foundation, 1998, p. 16.

[108] Cf. *White Paper on Intercultural Dialogue,* p. 3.

[109] Cf. Ibid., p. 15.

[110] Cf. Ibid.

cultivating a "culture of dialogue" or "spirit of dialogue". Intercultural dialogue can take place only in an environment where different views can be voiced openly, freely and without fear and where a person is guaranteed safety, dignity, equality of opportunity and participation. There should be legal or political recognition of minority cultures and their identities, basic human, civic, economic, social and cultural rights and institutions.

One should possess a good knowledge about the distinguishing features of one's own culture[111], and adequate knowledge of the culture of the partners in dialogue: provenience, history, dominant values, traditions, religious beliefs and practices, institutions, philosophies, theologies, etc. When speaking about intercultural dialogue Pope Benedict XVI says: "[...] a dialogue that, if it is to be effective, has to set out from a deep-seated knowledge of the specific identity of the various dialogue partners."[112]

None should be forced into dialogue but each participant should voluntarily choose to engage in dialogue. The partners in dialogue should manifest a mind-set characterised by openness, curiosity about the other and commitment, and the absence of a desire to "win" the dialogue or impose one's views on others. They should be open to the truth and manifest a desire to seek after it. One should be prepared to look at both similarities and differences found in cultures with a critical sense.

No sphere should be exempt from engaging in intercultural dialogue be it the neighbourhood, workplace, educational system, associated institutions, civil society and

---

[111] Hans Küng says that the one who conducts a dialogue with others without knowing his own position, confuses more than conveys. Cf. Hans Küng, *Spurensuche. Die Weltreligionen auf dem Weg*, München, Pieper, 2005, p. 301.

[112] Benedict XVI, Encyclical Letter *Caritas in Veritate* (29 June 2009), in *Acta Apostolicae Sedis*, 101 (2009), no. 26.

particularly the youth sector, the media, the world of arts and the political arena.[113] Since religious beliefs and practices are part of human life, religion should not be outside the sphere of intercultural dialogue because there is an intrinsic relationship between religion and culture and each religion is also a culture.

## 4. Aims of intercultural dialogue

One of the important aims of intercultural dialogue is reciprocal enrichment through a common search for the truth, the discovery of positive values in others, and the removal of prejudices, discrimination and exploitation of cultures that are weak. It can combat intolerance, social exclusion, racism, xenophobia, ethnocentrism, ghettoization, cultural hegemony and defend cultural identities.

Another objective of intercultural dialogue is to learn to live together peacefully and constructively in a culturally pluralistic world and develop a sense of community and belonging. Dialogue can help manage cultural diversity in a democratic manner by making the necessary adjustments to uphold the equality and dignity of all cultures. Thus dialogue can become a means to appreciate cultures and strengthen their identities.

Intercultural dialogue can contribute to political, social, cultural and economic integration and the cohesion of culturally diverse societies.[114] It can bridge the divide between those who perceive cultural diversity as a threat to social cohesion and national unity and those who view it as enrichment. Dialogue can help to share different worldviews, to understand and learn from those who see the world from different perspectives. Through dialogue one can also identify similarities and differences between various cultural

---

[113] Cf. *White Paper on Intercultural Dialogue*, p. 9.
[114] Cf. Ibid., p. 16.

traditions and perceptions.

Intercultural dialogue is meant to know each other better and their cultures, and do things together for the common good.Hence the recognition of common human needs across cultures is another aim of intercultural dialogue. It follows that for the sake of the common good people of different cultures need to make adjustments. Intercultural dialogue can also guarantee constant reflection on human rights and democratic principles and the functioning of democracies.

To search for common ethical values is another objective of intercultural dialogue. God is at work in every human being who, through reason, perceives the mystery of God and recognises universal values. Dialogue finds its *raison d'être* in searching for the patrimony of common ethical values found within the different religious traditions. In this way, believers can contribute to affirming the common good, justice and peace.[115]

Dialogue is a powerful instrument of mediation and reconciliation where conflicts exist. It can both prevent and resolve conflicts. More specifically, it is a means to achieve a consensus that conflicts should not be resolved by violence. Besides, through dialogue one can share with each other the best practices of cultures, particularly in the areas of democratic management of social diversity, conflict resolution, promotion of social cohesion and co-operation in joint projects.

Intercultural dialogue helps to respond to global challenges like wars, violence, terrorism, religious fundamentalism, narrow cultural nationalism, religious persecution, ethnic conflicts and environmental issues. It can promote the primacy of the human person, religious liberty, tolerance of diversity and different values in individuals,

---

[115] Cf. Congregation for Catholic Education, *Educating to intercultural dialogue in catholic schools*, no. 13.

institutions, communities, religions and nations. It can prevent the disappearance of cultures, which as Pope Francis says, can be just as serious, or even more serious than the disappearance of a species of plant or animal.[116]

Intercultural dialogue can help people co-exist and build up a civilisation of love based on understanding, respect and esteem for other cultures and their spiritual values.[117] It can contribute to purifying cultures from any dehumanising elements, and thus act as an agent of transformation. It can also help to uphold certain traditional cultural values, which are under threat from modernity and from globalisation.[118] Dialogue is also very important for one's own maturity because in encountering another person, other cultures, and other religions in the right way, one can grow, develop and mature.[119]

## 5. Theological foundations of intercultural dialogue

There are theological foundations for intercultural dialogue. This is especially important for Catholics because the Catholic Church is an ardent promoter of intercultural and interreligious dialogue. Below we present some of the theological foundations for dialogue between cultures:

---

[116] Cf. Francis, Encyclical Letter *Laudato si* (24 May 2015), Città del Vaticano, Libraria Editrice Vaticana, 2015, no. 145.

[117] Cf. Giovanni Paolo II, "*Dialogo tra le culture per una civiltà dell'amore e della pace*", no. 20.

[118] Cf. Pontificio Consiglio per il Dialogo Interreligioso e Congregazione per l'Evangelizzazione dei Popoli, "Dialogo e annuncio: Riflessioni e orientamenti sull'annuncio del vangelo e il dialogo interreligioso" (19 maggio 1991), in *Enchiridion Vaticanum. Documenti Ufficiali della Santa Sede 1991-1993*, Vol. 13, Testo ufficiale e versione Italiana, Bologna, Centro Editoriale Dehoniano, 1995, no. 46.

[119] Cf. Francis, *Speech to Students and Teachers of the Seibu Gakuen Bunri Junior High School of Saitama*, Tokyo, 21 August 2013 in https://w2.vatican.va/content/francesco/en/speeches/2013/august/documents/papa-francesco_20130821_collegio-saitama-giappone.html (1.5.2017)

*God is present in every culture*: In 1986 Pope John Paul II, during his visit to India, affirmed in one of his homilies the presence of God in cultures: "*God is present in the very heart of human cultures because he is present in man* [...]. God is present in the cultures of India. He has been present in all the peoples who have contributed by their experiences and aspirations to the formulations of those values, customs, institutions and arts which comprise the cultural heritage of this ancient land."[120]

*The Holy Spirit is at work in cultures:* The Spirit of God is the prime agent of the Church's dialogue with all peoples, cultures and religions.[121] In the encyclical *Redemptoris missio* Pope John Paul II stated that the presence and activity of the Spirit affect not only the individuals but also society and history, peoples, cultures and religions. The Spirit is at the origin of the noble ideals and undertakings, which benefit humanity on its journey through history. The Spirit of God directs the course of the ages and renews the face of the earth. The risen Christ is now at work in human hearts through the strength of his Spirit, not only instilling a desire for the world to come but also by animating, purifying and reinforcing the noble aspirations which drive the human family to make its life one that is more human and to direct the whole earth to this end. Again, it is the Spirit who sows the "seeds of the Word" present in various customs and cultures, preparing them for full maturity in Christ.[122] Whatever the Spirit brings about in human hearts and in the history of peoples, in cultures and religions serves as a preparation for the Gospel.[123]

---

[120] *Insegnamenti di Giovanni Paolo II*, Vol. IX, parte 1, Città del Vaticano, Libraria Editrice Vaticana, 1986, p. 269. (Italics in the original)

[121] Cf. John Paul II, Apostolic Exhortation *Ecclesia in Asia* (6 November 1999), in *Acta Apostolicae Sedis*, 92 (2000), no. 15.

[122] Cf. John Paul II, Encyclical Letter *Redemptoris missio* (7 December 1990), in *Acta Apostolicae Sedis*, 83 (1991), no. 28.

[123] Cf. John Paul II, *Ecclesia in Asia*, no. 16.

*Culture has an intrinsic capacity to receive divine revelation:* Pope John Paul II in *Fides et ratio* argued that all people are part of a culture, depend upon it and shape it. Human beings are both child and parent of the culture in which they are immersed. To everything they do, they bring something which sets them apart from the rest of creation: their unfailing openness to mystery and their boundless desire for knowledge. Lying deep in every culture, there appears this impulse towards a fulfilment. Hence we may say that culture itself has an intrinsic capacity to receive divine revelation.[124]

*There are elements that are good, true, and noble in cultures:* Pope Paul VI said that the Church is deeply rooted in the world, it exists in the world and draws its members from the world and it derives from it a wealth of human culture.[125] Pope Benedict XVI taught that God does not reveal himself in the abstract, but by using languages, imagery and expressions that are bound to different cultures.[126] Pope John Paul II affirmed that every group of people has its own native and seminal wisdom, which, as a true cultural treasure, tends to find voice and develop in forms which are genuinely philosophical.[127] On 18 December 1993 he told the bishops of Nigeria in *ad limina* visit: "By your continued study of all that is good, true, and noble in your peoples' cultures, it will become clearer how evangelisation can spread deeper roots among them."[128]

*Cultures offer different paths to the truth:* Cultures show forth the human being's characteristic openness to the

---

[124] Cf. John Paul II, Encyclical Letter *Fides et ratio* (14 September 1998), in *Acta Apostolicae Sedis*, 91 (1999), no. 71.

[125] Cf. Paul VI, Encyclical Letter *Ecclesiam suam* (6 August 1964), in *Acta Apostolicae Sedis,* 56 (1964), no. 26, p. 617.

[126] Cf. Benedict XVI, Apostolic Exhortation *Verbum Domini* (30 September 2010), in *Acta Apostolicae Sedis,* 102 (2010), no. 109.

[127] Cf. John Paul II, *Fides et ratio*, no. 3.

[128] *Insegnamenti di Giovanni Paolo II,* Vol. XVI parte 2, Citta del Vaticano, Libraria Editrice Vaticana, 1995, p. 1496.

universal and the transcendent. Therefore, they offer different paths to the truth which serve men and women in revealing values that can make their life ever more human.[129] Pope Benedict XVI adds: "Every authentic culture, if it is truly to be at the service of humanity, has to be open to transcendence and, in the end, to God."[130]

## 6. Anthropological foundations of intercultural dialogue

Intercultural dialogue has anthropological foundations. Pope Benedict XVI argued that the phenomenon of culture, in its multiple aspects, is an essential datum of human experience. This calls in the first place for a recognition of the importance of culture for the life of every person.[131] According to Pope John Paul II, human beings live always according to a culture which is properly theirs, and which in turn creates among persons a bond, which is properly theirs, one which determines the inter-human and social character of human existence.[132]

Christian anthropology places the basis of men and women and their ability to create culture in their being created in the image and likeness of God, a Trinity of Persons in communion. In addition, a man or a woman is not an isolated individual, but a *person*: a being who is essentially *relational*. Every human being is called to communion because of his or her nature, which is created in the image and likeness of God (Gen 1:26-27). The communion, which a human person is called to share always involves a double dimension: *vertical* (communion with God) and *horizontal*

---

[129] Cf. John Paul II, *Fides et ratio*, no. 70.

[130] Benedict XVI, *Verbum Domini*, no. 109.

[131] Cf. Benedict XVI, *Verbum Domini*, no. 109.

[132] Cf. John Paul II, *Address to UNESCO* (2 June 1980), in *Acta Apostolicae Sedis*, 72 (1980), no. 6, p. 738.

(communion with people).[133]

The experience of intercultural relationships can be understood only in the light of the inclusion of individuals and peoples in the *one human family*, founded on solidarity and on the fundamental values of justice and peace. This perspective is illuminated in a striking way by the relationship between the Persons of the Trinity within the one divine Substance. In the light of the revealed mystery of the Trinity, we understand that true openness does not mean loss of individual identity but profound interpenetration.[134] The Christian tradition, which upholds the unity of the human race is found primarily in the metaphysical interpretation of the *"humanum"* in which *relationality* is an essential element.[135]

In the context of culture, encounter with another always happens between two flesh-and-blood individuals. To go out from oneself and consider the world from a different point of view is not a denial of oneself, but, on the contrary, is necessary for enhancing one's own identity.[136] Today humanity appears much more interactive than in the past. The development of people depends, above all, on a recognition that the human race is a single family working together in true communion, not simply a group of subjects who happen to live side by side.[137] Therefore, in order to establish intercultural relationships correctly, a sound anthropological foundation is needed. This must take as its starting-point the fact that human beings are, in their most intimate nature

---

[133] Cf. Congregation for Catholic Education, *Educating to intercultural dialogue in catholic schools,* no. 34. In this context it is also suggested to read Bruno Bordignon, *Persona è relazione*, Soveria Mannelli, Rubbettino, 2013.

[134] Cf. Benedict XVI, *Caritas in Veritate*, no. 54.

[135] Cf. Ibid., no. 55.

[136] Cf. Congregation for Catholic Education, *Educating to intercultural dialogue in catholic schools,* no. 38.

[137] Cf. Benedict XVI, *Caritas in Veritate*, no. 53.

*relational beings* who can neither live nor develop their potential without being in relationship with others. Men and women are not just individuals, like self-sufficient monads, but are open and grow towards that which is different from them. Human beings are persons, beings in relationship, who understand themselves in relationship with others. This relationship arrives at its most profound level if it is based on love.[138] Besides, it is primarily not cultures but persons who enter into contact with each other – persons who are rooted in their own history and relationships.[139]

## 7. Forms of intercultural dialogue

Intercultural dialogue is a means of building openness, understanding and trust needed to live and cooperate with people of different cultures, despite their differences. It can take place in a variety of ways and at different levels and assume various forms. We can categorise the forms of intercultural dialogue as follows:

## 7.1. Dialogue of social life

The dialogue of social life consists of encounter of peoples belonging to diverse cultural backgrounds in their daily life and ordinary social relations. To live in a positive relationship with others who have different cultural identities as good neighbours, is the essence of this form of dialogue. Dialogue between cultures is not an exchange between cultural entities in the abstract but interaction between individuals who belong to different cultures. Besides, cultures can exist only through the people who represent them. Hence the dialogue of social life is the most basic and indispensable form of intercultural dialogue. It requires no special training in

---

[138] Cf. Congregation for Catholic Education, *Educating to intercultural dialogue in catholic schools,* no. 39.

[139] Cf. Ibid., no. 42.

dialogue; what matters is the good will to meet the other in a spirit of friendship.

Enrique Banús argues that, in a certain sense, every contact between human beings is an intercultural contact because culture is essentially linked to human beings, and we always carry our "cultural world" with us. Therefore all messages are cultural messages and all dialogues are intercultural dialogues.[140] In daily life we have contacts with other human beings "on the street", and we experience that, in such contacts, "our cultural world" is meeting other "cultural worlds".[141] Many intercultural encounters occur daily in various places such as in the street, in markets, while travelling, in work places, hospitals, schools, universities, sports clubs, youth centres, city squares and parks. Intercultural encounters also take place when people take part in the festivities of people belonging to other cultures such as marriage celebrations and funerals, when people exchange gifts during their religious festivals, invite others to dinner in their homes, offer help during moments of daily need and local events, play with the youth who are from different cultural backgrounds, or study in a school or university with students whose religions and cultures are different. These are all occasions for taking part in dialogue of social life.

In an intercultural encounter one's attitude towards others will be expressed not only verbally but also in non-verbal language: with the face, gestures, reactions, the way one looks, etc. Thus before the first word is said, an inner world is exteriorised and transmitted to the other.[142] When an encounter with another person with a different culture is

---

[140] Cf. Enrique Banús, "The Art of Intercultural dialogue", in *Intercultural Dialogue and Citizenship. Transmitting Values into Actions. A Common Project for Europeans and Their Partners*, Léonce Bekemans, Maria Karasinska-Fendler *et al* (eds.), Venice, Marsilio Editori, 2007, pp. 104-105.

[141] Cf. Ibid., p. 105.

[142] Cf. Ibid., p. 104.

positive, there is already an intercultural dialogue.

But not all intercultural encounters are true dialogues. One needs to make an effort to have a true dialogue. One needs to have a positive or at least an open attitude towards the other: wanting to listen, to know who the other is, and to be curious about the other's way of life. There are people who deliberately reject such encounters for fear of being influenced and losing their cultural identity. One can also consider his or her culture as superior to others and reject the meeting as not worthwhile or as a waste of time.

Formal education at school plays an eminent role in developing the consciousness of the need of overcoming mental blocks and establishing dialogue, and in creating "experts" of intercultural dialogue in daily life. But at the same time formal education alone is not enough. The influence of family plays a major role in it. Groups of friends can also be influenced considerably with regard to opinions and attitudes towards other cultures.[143] The dialogue of social life is part of the broader perspective of *creating a culture of dialogue,* which in the long run, can lead to deeper levels of dialogue between cultures.

## 7.2. Dialogue of good works

The dialogue of good works is co-operation between people belonging to different cultures for some common good. Co-operating and working together already implies a certain degree of trust and friendship between people, belief in their abilities, and the goodness found in them. To work for the common good also implies the acceptance of certain basic ethical values like honesty, truthfulness, equality, fairness in business dealings and respect for human dignity.

Often we come across volunteers who belong to different

---

[143] Cf. Ibid., p. 109.

cultures who are motivated by their religious convictions or simply by their desire to do good to others. They respond instinctively to people in need, manifest solidarity, and help the vulnerable and marginalised sections of people in society: poor and abandoned children, the sick, the old, physically impaired, refugees, immigrants, etc. People also manifest willingness to work together in the public sector: schools, public security, public health, fund raising for common projects, disaster management, initiating public debates for the common good, presence in the media to promote cultural values and cultural integration.

The collaboration of individuals and groups with local governments for the common good are tangible expressions of the dialogue of good works. The formation of associations, clubs, voluntary organisations for the economic, social and cultural welfare of people, political participation, sports activities, music and cultural shows, placing at the disposal of people in need certain edifices belonging to religious groups and institutions and so on are also manifestations of dialogue of good works.

Often the non-governmental civil society actors are the driving force in promoting the dialogue of good works. Sometimes they are local neighbourhood associations, minority or migrant agencies, religious organisations and charitable institutions. They work, for example, to defend human rights, to protect religious and ethnic minorities, and to defend the rights of marginalised men and women against prejudice, racism, discrimination, stereotypes and ethnocentrism. These entities are powerful agents in breaking down walls between cultures and promoting dialogue.

## 7.3. Dialogue of cultural experts

The dialogue of cultural experts is a scholarly exchange between professionals on matters related to culture. It is a dialogue carried out between intellectuals, academicians, scholars, researchers and other experts on culture. Over the centuries, many individual cultural professionals and private organisations have made great contributions to this form of dialogue.

In a dialogue of cultural experts, the participants discuss a wide range of matters related culture such as art, literature, architecture, philosophy, history, archaeology, anthropology, ethnology, religions, theology, ethics, sociology, science, technology, digital divide, etc. They undertake cross-cultural comparative studies, engage in research, organise symposiums, seminars and conferences, and publish scholarly literature on matters related to culture. Through their interventions, they educate the public on cultural matters, create among them an awareness of cultural pluralism and its advantages and disadvantages. They challenge the prevailing stereotypes about certain cultures and work to promote cultural identity and the acceptance of cultural differences. They identify cultural conflicts and suggest solutions to overcome them.

The cultural experts explore the role that education and mass media play in fostering intercultural dialogue. They influence public opinion through their presence in the media. They identify opportunities for the promotion of cultures at regional, national and international levels. They share successful experiences and initiatives that have contributed to the promotion of policies and programmes related to fostering a culture of dialogue. They influence the cultural policies of governments and offer practical recommendations for the promotion of intercultural dialogue by governmental and non-governmental organisations, academic institutions, media and civil society organizations. Thus they play a vital role in fostering a "spirit of dialogue" between cultures.

## 7.4. Civil dialogue

Civil dialogue refers to the exchange of ideas about public

issues and policies or decisions, which may have consequences that affect people's lives, communities, and society as a whole. The main field of civil dialogue is the *political milieu.*

Civil dialogue is an important aspect of democracy, and the common good is its objective. The purpose of this form of dialogue is to implement the democratisation of institutions in policies and decision-making processes. The stress is on openness, participation, consensus-building, collaborative decision-making and collective accountability. It calls for the art of listening and respect for the views of those with whom one may disagree.

Meaningful civil dialogue is intentional and purposeful, and addresses matters of public importance. It can increase the capacity of communities to respond intelligently and with practical sense to the changing environments around them and help them handle crises with ease. Civil dialogue tries to involve all sections of people: ordinary citizens from grassroots, business people, industrialists, academicians, researchers, religious leaders, representatives of associations and organisations, political parties and government agencies. In some countries there are ministries with sector-specific portfolios in the fields of education, youth, culture, sport, tourism, religious affairs and human resource development.

In multicultural societies, cultural issues are an important part of civil dialogue on topics dealing with migrants, refugees, ethnic and religious minorities, building churches, temples, mosques, synagogues, cultural integration, intercultural education, managing ethnic conflicts, etc.

Civil dialogue contributes to social cohesion and finds solutions to local or regional issues and bring about sustainable rural and urban development. It works on the principle of the new understanding of leadership, which fosters a climate of dialogue, participation and decentralisation. In promoting civil dialogue one should be sensitive to people's belief systems and cultural traditions.

## 7.5. Dialogue of diplomacy

Diplomacy is essentially a political activity, well-resourced and skilful, and a major component of power. Its principal objective is to enable States to secure the objective of their *foreign policies* without resorting to force, propaganda or law. Diplomacy consists of communication between officials designed to promote foreign policy. Diplomacy is not merely what professional diplomatic agents do. It is carried out by other officials and by private persons under the direction of officials.[144] There are ministries of foreign affairs or Departments of State, embassies and consulates that engage in dialogues of diplomacy. They use conferences, summits, propaganda, disguised embassies, special missions and mediation to achieve their goals. In all this what is common is *diplomatic dialogue*. Through this form of dialogue countries are committed to contribute to peace and security, to prevent, manage and resolve violent conflicts and to promote stable and democratic political environments.

Intercultural dialogue is an emerging issue in international diplomacy. Multicultural issues are crucial governance issues not only at local and national levels but also at an international level. The dialogue of diplomacy is implemented in order to improve international democracy, promote human rights, public policies, find solutions to problems concerning refugees and asylum seekers and immigrants, and to prevent wars and conflicts. Today diplomatic dialogue has become a comprehensive dialogue on a broad range of issues: politics, economics, military matters and security, terrorism, illicit drugs, human rights, racial and religious discrimination, religious fundamentalism, genocide,

---

[144] Cf. G. R. Berridge, *Diplomacy. Theory and Practice*, New York, Palgrave Macmillan, 2010, p. 1.

regional issues and areas of co-operation.

The dialogue of diplomacy is very important in instances involving immigrants and refugees who come from different cultural and religious backgrounds. A typical example is the diplomacy of the European Union in handling the huge influx of immigrants and refugees from the Middle East and Africa since 2014. Today, the European countries are trying to handle this emergency situation through a series of diplomatic dialogues. Some of the other areas where serious diplomatic dialogue is in progress among the leading nations of the world involve problems concerning international terrorism, especially ISIS (ISIL), and climatic change.

## 7.6. Dialogue of ethics

All cultures have an ethical component: it is part of the wisdom common to all cultures. Ethics deals with rightness and wrongness in human behaviour and the promotion of certain values, and is oriented towards helping people to lead a good, orderly and meaningful life. It is guided by an overall pledge to safeguard justice, truth, human dignity and human rights, and build harmonious relationships between individuals and within societies.

Since ethics is integral to all cultures, ethical issues enter into intercultural dialogue. Ethical conduct is a component of human interaction, and the need for it increases when relationships occur across cultures. Ethical values of the different cultures can be a common ground for initiating a dialogue between them. But cultural diversity also manifests ethical diversity, and ethical differences across cultures are real. An ethical issue can give rise to conflict of values.

Intercultural dialogue requires careful attention to ethics. One of the biggest debates in the field of intercultural relations is in the area of ethics. The basic questions are: can one apply the same ethical criteria to all cultures, or whether each culture can determine for itself what is right and wrong? These and similar matters have been debated by philosophers, sociologists, anthropologists and experts on cultures and promoters of intercultural dialogue for a long time. Some argue for a meta-ethics, which holds that there is some overarching ethical ideal or system that can be applied to all cultures. Some others subscribe to cultural relativism, which argues that each culture determines on its own what is right and wrong. The first approach implies that there are certain ethical principles that guide the behaviour of peoples of different cultures. In fact, most intercultural scholars today believe that there are certain universal principles and values found in each culture. Only a few would argue that anything a culture does is equally right as any other behaviour.

Intercultural dialogue based on ethics is needed to become aware of the different ethical values of cultures. Such a dialogue can lead to the discovery of the foundations of ethics among cultures and the ethical principles that regulate a society's relationships. A dialogue of ethics is essential for constructing a better world: to work for human rights, liberty, justice, peace, equality, solidarity, tolerance, protection of the earth, a culture of non-violence and respect for every form of life. In an ethical dialogue people of all walks of life can participate, and its aim is to discover universal ethical norms and values, identify the ethical differences, and if possible, correct and purify what is not in agreement with respecting human dignity and human rights.

The famous theologian Hans Küng in his search of a "global ethic" (*Weltethos*) argues for the need for consensus on certain values, standards and basic moral attitudes among cultures and religions. He defines "global ethic" as a minimal consensus concerning binding values, irrevocable standards and fundamental moral attitudes.[145] According to him, there can be no survival of our planet without a global ethic.[146] The principles of global ethic can be affirmed by all people with ethical convictions, whether religiously grounded or not. The global ethic values are immutable, fundamental and universal. Without an ethical consensus a community will sooner or later succumb to chaos or dictatorship. Without a world ethic there cannot be order in the world.[147] This was fully endorsed by the World Parliament of Religions held in Chicago from 28 August to 4 September 1993 and in which about 6,500 people of all possible religions participated. The assembly approved a document on global ethic entitled "The Declaration of a Global Ethic". This was done because among the religions there is a certain consensus with regard to ethics. The declaration presented the following as immutable ethical norms: a) the need for a culture of non-violence and respect for all forms of life; b) the need for a culture of solidarity and a just economic order; c) the need for a culture of tolerance and a life founded on sincerity; and (d) the necessity of a culture of equality of rights and solidarity between men and women.[148]

Another document that stresses the importance of a global ethic is the "Declaration of Human Responsibilities." It was proposed by the InterAction Council in 1997 and proclaimed by the General Assembly of the United Nations as a common standard for all peoples and all nations. It has 19 articles that deal with the following themes: fundamental principles for humanity, non-violence and respect for life, justice and solidarity, truthfulness and tolerance and mutual respect and

---

[145] Cf. Hans Küng e Karl-Josef Kuschel, *Per un'etica mondiale. La dichiarazione del parlamento delle religioni mondali*, Giovanni Moretto (tr.), Milano, Rizzoli, 1995, p. 18.

[146] He says: "*Kein Überleben unsres Globus ohne ein globales Ethos, ein Weltethos.*" Hans Küng, *Spurensuche*, p. 16.

[147] Cf. Hans Küng e Karl-Josef Kuschel, *Per un'etica mondiale*, p. 7.

[148] Cf. Ibid., pp. 8, 27-37.

partnership.[149] Hans Küng says that both the declarations are addressed to both believers and non-believers, that they are aimed at everyone and that they can be shared by theologians, philosophers, mystics, agnostics, Christians and followers of other religions.[150]

## 7.7. Dialogue of religion

By "dialogue of religion" we mean a dialogue based on the cultural and social implications of religion. There is an intimate relationship between religion and culture and they mutually influence each other. Religion is an important ally in intercultural dialogue, and if it is left out, an essential dimension of culture will be missing. If religion is an integral aspect of culture, intercultural dialogue cannot neglect religion. Besides, religion is an integral part of human life, and therefore it cannot be outside the sphere of cultural dialogue. There is also evidence of the recession of the secularisation process in many contemporary societies and the affirmation of religious beliefs. This is an additional reason to promote dialogue of religion.

For a long time, some people who were actively engaged in intercultural dialogue showed reluctance to take religion into account because of the divide between public life and religion as a consequence of the so-called secularisation paradigm which regards religion as an irrelevant or utterly negative factor. But now things are changing and people are realising more and more the value of religion in intercultural dialogue.

Religion always has two aspects: one is in the direction of

---

[149] Cf. "Dichiarazione Universale delle Responsabilità dell'Uomo", in *Ethos mondiale e globalizzazione*, Gerardo Cunico, Karl-Josef Kuschel e Domenico Venturelli (a cura di), Genova, Il Melangolo, 2005, pp. 31-35.

[150] Cf. Hans Küng, "Un Confronto fra i due documenti", in *Ethos mondiale e globalizzazione*, Gerardo Cunico, Karl-Josef Kuschel e Domenico Venturelli (a cura di), Genova, Il Melangolo, 2005, p. 41.

*religious identity* so that a person considers himself or herself as belonging to a particular religion: thus one is a Buddhist, Christian, Jew, Hindu, Muslim, Sikh, Jain, follower of a traditional religion or any other faith; the other aspect is in the direction of *morality and ethics*: the great religions are able to transcend particular identities and produce desires in people for moral and ethical life.

The field of the dialogue of religion is very vast, and it can deal with such matters as: the relationship between religion and culture, and politics, religion and economics, religion and psychiatry, the role of religion in public life, religion and ecology, religious liberty and freedom of conscience, gender identity and religion, place and role of religious minorities in society, religion and ethics, religion and law, religion and science, religion and international diplomacy, the importance of engaging religious leaders and institutions in advancing human development, religion and human rights, religion and conflict mitigation, the need for religion to be purified by reason, religion and mass media, religious education in schools and universities, etc.

The dialogue of religion can deal with such social problems such as the secularisation process which relegates religion to the private sphere and denies its role in public life, the problem of religious indifference which is widespread in many societies, the question of agnosticism, atheism, the resurgence of neo-paganism, the New Age movement, the issue of religious conversion, manipulation of religion for political ends, religious persecution, religious fundamentalism, religiously motivated terrorism, etc.

Religion has a natural place in the public sphere. Though many are in favour of separating religion from public life, civil authorities cannot deny the importance of dialogue with religious communities, religious institutions and religious leaders to facilitate cultural integration in a locality, region or nation. In fact, in some societies constructive religious dialogue is an essential element of the promotion of human rights and social harmony. Sometimes religion is seen as an obstacle to peaceful co-existence and social cohesion, and this can become a relevant theme for intercultural dialogue. Another important theme for dialogue is the relationship between religion and State – whether the two should be related at all, and if they are related, how and in what way. Also what are the possible positive and negative aspects of such a relationship or the effects of the negation of such a relationship.

Today religious issues are a decisive part of much of international diplomacy. Religion and peace has a close relationship. Raimon Panikkar argues that, from time immemorial war has constituted a religious problem, peace is eminently a religious affair, and today political peace is rediscovering its religious roots.[151] The role of religion in conflict and in conflict resolution is widely recognised. Often behind a cultural conflict there is a religious dimension. In some cases of conflicts religion is the central factor but misreported as primarily racial, regional or colonial.[152] In many parts of the world, religion should be seen as a central political pillar maintaining the power of any ruler, a major factor in determining the people's loyalty, and a key ingredient in determining a nation's stability or instability.[153] Hence it is argued that, the secret of the influence of religion in contemporary world politics is that, the modernisation process, rather than causing religion to weaken and disappear, often makes its public role stronger and a more necessary part of the process of State building or revolutionary

---

[151] Cf. Raimon Panikkar, *Cultural Disarmament. The Way to Peace*, Louisville, Westminster John Knox Press, 1995, pp. 29,33,53.

[152] Cf. Edward Luttwak, "The Missing Dimension", in *Religion, the Missing Dimension of Statecraft*, Douglas Johnston and Cynthia Sampson (eds.), Oxford, Oxford University Press, 1994, p. 11.

[153] Cf. Barry Rubin, "Religion and International Affairs", in *Religion, the Missing Dimension of Statecraft*, Douglas Johnston and Cynthia Sampson (eds.), Oxford, Oxford University Press, 1994, pp. 20-21.

transformation.[154] Given the lack of other strong social institutions, the church or mosque and their clerical hierarchies and laypeople come to play an important function. They define values, social goals, and foreign relations. They also provide a base of support for the rulers or a foundation for the opposition.[155]

Dialogue among two or more religions traditions is known as interreligious dialogue, and it is situated within the religious dimension of culture. In the context of intercultural dialogue, interreligious dialogue must be viewed in terms of its *cultural and social implications*. In this way one avoids considering religion merely as a matter of faith but takes it in a broad sense to consider it as part of the common cultural heritage of people without it colliding with the individual beliefs of community members. None can deny the social significance of religion. Though the secularisation process is spreading in many cultures and every religion is affected by it, religion itself continues to be a living force in the lives of people who live within it.[156]

There are various ways in which religious believers can dialogue among themselves: there is the *dialogue of life* with its sharing of joys and sorrows, the *dialogue of works* with its collaboration in promoting the development of people, the *theological dialogue*, when this is possible, with the study of each other's religious heritage and the *dialogue of religious experience*.[157] These activities are also within the larger framework of intercultural dialogue.

Dialogue among religions can be conducted with civic

---

[154] Cf. Ibid., p. 23.

[155] Cf. Ibid., p. 24.

[156] Cf. Conferenza dei vescovi cattolici d'Inghilterra e Galles, "Incontrare Dio nell'amico e nello straniero", in *Il Regno*, Documenti 11 (2010), p. 359.

[157] Cf. Congregation for Catholic Education, *Educating to intercultural dialogue in catholic schools,* no. 14.

matters also. Leaders and followers of different religions can meet and work on a common project. Such a project can serve, for instance, to ensure peace and social harmony, to manage religious differences, to make decisions on projects in rural and urban areas, to help educational institutions, associations, public bodies, etc. Hence it is important to recognise the social, political and cultural relevance of interreligious dialogue.

## 8. Importance of intercultural education for intercultural dialogue

Education is the process of teaching and learning in order to acquire knowledge, skills, values, attitudes and competencies required to become a responsible member of society. Education is at the heart of intercultural dialogue, and its aim is cultural integration. Intercultural education, both formal and informal, theoretical and practical, is designed to prepare the young generation to live in a culturally pluralistic society, respecting human dignity and human rights. It aims to promote justice, tolerance, mutual respect, understanding and openness to individuals and groups with different cultural, ethnic, national or religious backgrounds, and to combat prejudice, discrimination, and stereotypes, and resolve conflicts where necessary. It also provides teachers with additional professional skills needed to work effectively in culturally and ethnically mixed classrooms and to be cultural mediators. This form of education becomes especially important in an increasingly global and interdependent world, where encountering people from different cultures is unavoidable, and where reciprocity and complementarity of cultures are envisaged as positive values.[158]

---

[158] UNESCO has identified four roles of intercultural education: a) learning to know, b) learning to do, c) learning to live together, and (d)

Designing the *curricula* is very important for intercultural education; it should take into consideration the existing cultural situation of the territory. It should be inclusive to highlight the cultural diversity,and avoid any content that is of discriminatory nature. Intercultural education goes beyond the formalities of textbook learning and focuses also on *informal intercultural learning activities*. In intercultural education *language learning* is given importance so that minorities and immigrants learn and practice the official language of the country where they live. Cordial, open and respectful *teacher-student relationships* can also promote intercultural dialogue. It is true that in intercultural education the main target is children and youth. But there are also several *other groups,* which need to be addressed simultaneously if intercultural dialogue is to succeed. They are: school administrators, non-teaching staff, local civil authorities, media persons, parents and other close relatives,.[159]

---

learning to be. Cf. http://unesdoc.unesco.org/ images/ 0014/ 001478/147878e.pdf (1.5.2017)

[159] For a good treatment of some of the themes related to intercultural education one may profitably read: Michele Pellerey, "Globalizzazione e problemi educativi nella società multiculturale", in *Educare nella Multiculturalità*, Vito Orlando (a cura di), Roma, LAS, 2003, pp. 15-33; Cyril De Souza, "Educazione etico/religiosa in un contesto multireligioso", in *Educare nella Multiculturalità*, Vito Orlando (a cura di), Roma, LAS, 2003, pp. 37-46; Natale Zanni, "La scuola in un contesto multiculturale e didattica interculturale", in *Educare nella Multiculturalità*, Vito Orlando (a cura di), Roma, LAS, 2003, pp. 61-67; Vito Orlando, "L'educazione interculturale: significati e prospettive pedagogiche di realizzazione" in *Educare nella Multiculturalità*, Vito Orlando (a cura di), Roma, LAS, 2003, pp. 95-121; Id., *Attenzione ai migranti e missione Salesiana nelle società multiculturale d'Europa*, Roma, LAS, 2012, pp. 35-56; Gigliola Corduas, "L'interculturalità nei banchi di scuola", in *La Sfida di babele. Incontri e sconti nelle società multicultuirali,* Elena Bein Ricco (a cura di), Torino, Claudina, 2001, pp. 39-66.

## 9. Challenges to intercultural dialogue

Though intercultural dialogue is spoken of often and widely practiced, there are many challenges to it. The dialogue of cultures is not an answer to all cultural problems and social evils, and therefore its scope is limited. It is impossible to dialogue with one who refuses to dialogue. Even if the parties are willing to dialogue, they may differ in their values and one may need a longer process of interaction to reach certain agreement and implementation of the values of human rights, democracy and the rule of law.[160] Today, many people are uncritically absorbing cultural elements from different cultures, and in the process they seem to possess a "hybrid identity" or "multiple cultural identities", and this may not be suitable for any serious intercultural dialogue. Another obstacle to dialogue is cultural eclecticism where cultures are simply placed alongside one another and viewed as substantially equivalent and interchangeable.[161] Cultural relativism is another obstacle to dialogue where cultures co-exist side by side and remain separate with no authentic dialogue and no true integration.[162] The tendency towards monoculturalism, which tries to impose one culture on all people is opposed to the spirit of dialogue. Both secularism and fundamentalism exclude the possibility of fruitful dialogue and effective co-operation between cultures. There are people who argue that religious identity is an obstacle to intercultural dialogue and they want to ignore it. In some countries religion and State are so intertwined that it gives preference to one religion and denies the right of existence to other religions or they are constantly persecuted. In other countries some ethnic groups are denied their right to preserve their cultural identity. In certain cultures involving women in intercultural dialogue is problematic, as for them,

---

[160] Cf. *White Paper on Intercultural Dialogue*, p. 16.
[161] Cf. Benedict XVI, *Caritas in veritate*, no. 26.
[162] Cf. Ibid.

equality between men and women does not exist. Identifying competent individuals and agencies for intercultural dialogue and giving them a suitable formation is also a great challenge. Bitter and humiliating historic memories of certain cultures can also be a problem in intercultural dialogue.

## 10. The Catholic Church and intercultural dialogue

The Catholic Church by its very nature is multicultural, and it is constantly in dialogue with other cultures. For a Christian, to dialogue with cultures means to obey the commandment of Christ to love one's neighbour (Lk 10:25-37). In order to understand the attitude of the Church towards cultures and intercultural dialogue, it is important to refer to Vatican Council II. The Church realised that it was called to participate in the creation of a new world through self-renewal and dialogue with the world. This resulted in a great sense of openness towards cultural pluralism. The Council discovered a world in its diversity of mentalities and cultures, which was concretely manifested in the presence of bishops from all over the world. It was the first time that a Council had a consistent number of bishops from the so-called third world. It listened to the points of view of bishops from the Churches of Asia, Africa and Latin American countries, which produced a great impact in the Council. The representatives from Eastern Europe made the Council aware of the crude reality of the world of Communism. Along with the bishops, other participants (specialists, representatives of religious congregations and laity, and ecumenical observers) also contributed to the openness of the Church towards cultural pluralism. This led to a new ecclesial perception of cultures. It is especially seen in the document *Gaudium et spes* (Joy and hope) which is the Pastoral Constitution of

Vatican Council II on the Church in the modern world. [163] The articles 53-62 of this document contain the main teachings of the Vatican II on culture.[164]

In order to promote dialogue between cultures the Catholic Church encourages the creation of cultural centres. The Cultural Commissions (or Committees) of the Church are excellent tools for the dialogue of cultures, and Bishops' Conferences are asked to establish them where they do not already exist.[165] Today, in many places, Catholic cultural centres are a rich and varied phenomenon and they carry out intercultural dialogue in a variety of ways.[166]

## 10.1. Role of Pontifical Council for Culture

The Pontifical Council for Culture is an important Vatican department, which is responsible for the promotion of intercultural dialogue. The history of the Council dates back to Vatican Council II in the sense that, as said above, a whole section of the document *Gaudium et spes* emphasises the fundamental importance of culture for the full development of the human person, the many ways in which salvation and culture are linked, and the mutual enrichment of the Church and cultures throughout the history of civilisations. Building on the riches inherited from Pope Paul VI, Vatican Council II and the Synod of Bishops, Pope John Paul II founded the Pontifical Council for Culture in 1982.[167] His apostolic constitution *"Pastor bonus"* of 28 June 1988 gave further

---

[163] Cf. Hervé Carrier, *Dizionario della Cultura per l'analisi culturale e l'inculturazione*, Città del Vaticano, Libreria Editrice Vaticana, 1997, pp. 454-455, 457.

[164] Cf. Vatican Council II, Pastoral Constitution *Gaudium et spes* (7 Dicember 1965), in *Acta Apostolicae Sedis*, 58 (1966), nos. 53-62.

[165] Cf. Pontifical Council for Culture, *Towards a Pastoral Approach to Culture*, Città del Vaticano, Libraria Editrice Vaticana, 1999, no. 25.

[166] Cf. Ibid., no. 32.

[167] Cf. John Paul II, *Personal Letter to the Cardinal Secretary of State* (20 May 1982), in *Acta Apostolicae Sedis*, 74 (1982), pp. 683-688.

guidelines for the functioning of the Council.[168] On 25 March 1993 through his Motu Proprio *"Inde a Pontificatus"* he merged the Pontifical Council for Dialogue with Non-Believers (founded in 1965 by Paul VI) with the Pontifical Council for Culture.[169] On 11 March 2006 Pope Benedict XVI attached the Pontifical Council for Interreligious Dialogue with the Pontifical Council for Culture.[170] But on 1 September 2007 the former was detached from the latter, and once again made autonomous.[171]

### 10.1.1. The structure of the Council

The Pontifical Council for Culture has two sections: a) *Faith and Culture* b) *Dialogue with Cultures.*[172] The day-to-day work of the Council is entrusted to the *permanent staff* resident in Rome. The Council has a *plenary assembly* at least once every three years. The Council also relies on a group of *consultors* for the study of particularly important questions on culture.

### 10.1.2. The aims and tasks of the Council

The Pontifical Council for Culture assists the Pope in the exercise of his pastoral office for the benefit of the universal Church and of particular Churches concerning the encounter between the message of the Gospel and cultures, often marked by unbelief or religious indifference. It is also concerned with the relationships of the Church and the Holy See with the world of culture, and in particular it promotes

---

[168] Cf. John Paul II, Apostolic Constitution *"Pastor bonus"* (28 June 1988), in *Acta Apostolicae Sedis,* 80 (1988), arts. 166-168.

[169] Cf. John Paul II, Motu Proprio *"Inde a Pontificatus"* (25 March 1993), in *Insegnamenti di Giovanni Paolo II,* Vol. XVI parte 1, Citta del Vaticano, Libraria Editrice Vaticana, 1993, pp. 747-750.

[170] Cf. *L'Osservatore Romano,* 12 marzo 2007, p. 1.

[171] Cf. *L'Osservatore Romano,* 25-26 giugno 2007, p. 1.

[172] Cf. John Paul II, *"Inde a Pontificatus"*, art. 4, pp. 749-750.

dialogue with contemporary cultures. It oversees and co-ordinates the activities of the Pontifical Academies, and co-operates with the Pontifical Commission for the Cultural Heritage of the Church. It enters into dialogue with Bishops' Conferences, and Conferences of Major Religious Superiors in order to allow the whole Church to benefit from its initiatives on culture. It co-operates with Catholic universities and international organisations of a cultural, historical, philosophical, theological, scientific, artistic or intellectual nature, and keeps in touch with the activities of international bodies like the United Nations Educational, Scientific and Cultural Organization (UNESCO), the Council of Europe, and the cultural policies and activities of governments.[173]

## 10.2. Other Vatican departments that promote intercultural dialogue

Besides the Pontifical Council for Culture, the Holy See has other departments which also promote intercultural dialogue in ways specific to their nature of service, and among them two deserve special mention: The *Pontifical Council for Justice and Peace*,[174] which works for the promotion of justice, peace, and human rights from the perspective of the Catholic Church, and the *Pontifical Council for the Pastoral Care of Migrants and Itinerant People*.[175] Among other activities, it organises programmes of

---

[173] Cf. John Paul II, *Personal Letter to the Cardinal Secretary of State*, pp. 683-688; Id., "*Pastor bonus*", arts. 166-168; Id., "*Inde a Pontificatus*", arts. 1-4, pp. 747-750.

[174] On 6 January 1967 with the Motu Proprio "*Catholicam Christi Ecclesiam*" Pope Paul VI founded the Pontifical Commission for Justice and Peace. Cf. Paul VI, Motu Proprio "*Catholicam Christi Ecclesiam*" (6 January 1967), in *Acta Apostolicae Sedis*, 59 (1967), pp. 25-28.

[175] On 19 March 1970, with the Motu Proprio "*Apostolicae Caritatis*", Pope Paul VI established the "*Pontificia Commissio de Spirituali Migratorum atque Itinerantium Cura*", Cf. Paul VI, Motu Proprio "*Apostolicae Caritatis*" (19 March 1970), in *Acta Apostolicae Sedis*, 62 (1970), pp. 193-197.

action to promote non-discrimination against refugees and migrants in various parts of the world, to condemn racism and foster openness to immigrants. By the Motu Proprio *"Humanam Progressionem"* of 17 August 2016, Pope Francis instituted the Dicastery for Promoting Integral Human Development, and the Pontifical Council for Justice and Peace and the Pontifical Council for the Pastoral Care of Migrants and Itinerant People were merged with it, along with two others (the Pontifical Council *Cor Unum*, and the Pontifical Council for Health Care Workers). It took effect, *ad experimentum*, on 1 January 2017.[176]

## 11. Conclusion

Intercultural dialogue is at the heart of a civilised way of living in a multicultural world. Engaging in dialogue of cultures is the duty of every citizen, and it is meant for all people. For a Christian it is a concrete way of manifesting one's love for his or her neighbour. The aim of dialogue is the discovery and appreciation of cultural diversity, awareness of the positive values in others and respect for the full implementation of human, civic, economic, social and cultural rights. Cultural pluralism and differences are not *per se* a threat, rather a means for enrichment, a gift and a strength.[177] Intercultural dialogue is not a state of fact but a *process*, often complex and long, which requires time and patience for listening and understanding. It is here that education to multiculturalism becomes indispensable for society. In dialogue of cultures it is important to avoid cultural syncretism and eclecticism. It should uphold the right to be culturally different and not to become a victim of cultural levelling. Dialogue is fundamental to avoid cultural

---

[176] Cf. *L'Osservatore Romano*, 2 September 2016, English edition, p. 2.

[177] Cf. Theo Sommer, "Dialog der Kulturen: Von Identität und Integration, Pluralismus und Toleranz", in *Zukunft* der *Religionen*, Wolfgang Shultheiß (hrsg.), Frankfurt am Main, S. Fischer, 2003, p. 121.

conflicts. It is necessary for civil administration and the politics of governance, which have to deal with cultural diversity, equality and participation. Christianity is a culture but cultural pluralism is at the heart of the Church. The path of dialogue becomes possible and fruitful when it is based on the awareness of each individual's dignity and of the unity of all people in a common humanity, with the aim of sharing and building together a common destiny. On 18 January 1983 Pope John Paul II said in his speech to the plenary session of the Pontifical Council for Culture: "The more he [read "man" or "woman"] suffocates the dialogue of cultures, the more the modern world is caught up in conflicts that risk being lethal for the future of the human civilization."[178]

---

[178] John Paul II, *Speech to the Plenary Session of the Pontifical Council for Culture* (18 January 1983), in *Insegnamenti di Giovanni Paolo II*, Vol. VI parte 1, Citta del Vaticano, Libraria Editrice Vaticana, 1983, no. 7, p. 151.

# CONCLUSION

Culture is a complex concept. It is the totality of human experiences acquired, inherited, shared and transmitted from one generation to another. It consists of beliefs, customs, traditions, practices, attitudes, values, norms, ideas, artefacts, signs, symbols, languages and behaviour patterns. It covers the material and the spiritual. It is both stable and dynamic. All human beings have culture, and they are also producers of culture.

Culture is central to human life. One's way of life, principles and ideologies are products of one's culture. Culture influences one's perceptions, moral values and outlook to life. It shapes personalities and character, and gives one a sense of identity, self-worth and dignity.

Cultural diversity is a fundamental condition of human society. It is the result of globalisation, migration, growing interdependence between peoples and nations and the influence of mass media and social communications. In the face of cultural pluralism several negative attitudes are possible, such as, prejudice, discrimination, racism, xenophobia, ethnocentrism, ghettoization, denial of human and cultural rights, attempts to impose monoculturalism and cultural conflicts.

Intercultural dialogue is an essential dimension of managing cultural pluralism. It enables people to live together peacefully and constructively in a multicultural world and develop a sense of community and belonging through mutual acceptance and cultural integration. It is a means for the recognition of cultural identities and nation building. The practice of intercultural dialogue can build relationships and bring about new social and political policies conducive to promote justice and peace. It can help to foster international understanding and enable people to accept cultural differences with ease, and act as an antidote to cultural discrimination. Intercultural dialogue is crucial in preventing cultural conflicts and promoting reconciliation in the aftermath of conflicts. It must be based on the principles of the universality and inviolability of human rights, democracy and the rule of law.

Religions are also cultures. Religion and culture mutually influence each other. Therefore, it is necessary to involve religions in intercultural dialogue, and civil society organisations and world religious leaders are to strengthen their commitment to intercultural dialogue at local, national and international levels.

Education to intercultural dialogue is indispensable for all. It can be formal or informal and it should prepare people to live in a society that is culturally pluralistic and helps them to develop the skills and competence necessary for fruitful dialogue. It should also help them to see one's own culture through different eyes and carry out constructive self-criticism. All educational institutions, especially schools, universities, cultural centres and religious institutions, are privileged places where people can be given education to correct cultural relations and intercultural dialogue. Mass media and social communications also have a vital role in the promotion of objective knowledge about cultures, cultural integration and the dialogue of cultures.

In many educational institutions there is an urgent need to revise the curriculum of studies to meet the rapid cultural changes taking place in the world. Studies related to culture and the techniques and skills of intercultural dialogue need to be made mandatory in the curriculum for children, youth, adults and families and in the training of teachers, social workers, religious leaders, politicians, diplomats and media persons. While some educational institutions offer advanced courses in cultural studies and intercultural dialogue, unfortunately, a monoculture approach to education and formation of the young is still maintained by some countries, governments, world religions and educational institutions. Finally, there is a need to increase the number of intercultural institutions, associations and organisations and to make the existing ones function more efficiently. Better synergy between them is also needed in order to promote knowledge of cultures, cultural integration and intercultural dialogue.

# BIBLIOGRAPHY

"Dichiarazione Universale delle Responsabilità dell'Uomo", in *Ethos mondiale e globalizzazione*, Gerardo Cunico, Karl-Josef Kuschel e Domenico Venturelli (a cura di), Genova, Il Melangolo, 2005. 29-35.

Alleyne Brian, "'Race' and Racism", in *Encyclopedia of Social Theory*, Austin Harrington, Barbara I. Marshall and Hans-Peter Müller, London, Routledge, 2006, 490-492.

Bandyopadhyay Sekhar, "Caste", in *Encyclopedia of Social Theory*, Austin Harrington, Barbara I. Marshall and Hans-Peter Müller (eds.), London, Routledge, 2006, 48-50.

Banús, Enrique, "The Art of Intercultural dialogue", in *Intercultural Dialogue and Citizenship. Transmitting Values into Actions. A Common Project for Europeans and Their Partners*, Léonce Bekemans, Maria Karasinska-Fendler *et al* (eds.), Venice, Marsilio Editori, 2007, 101-112.

*Bibliography*

Banton Michael, "Assimilation", in *Dictionary of Race and Ethnic Relations*, E. Ellis Cashmore, Michael Banton, *et al*, (eds.), London, Routledge, 1988, 25-27.

Benedict XVI, Encyclical Letter *Caritas in Veritate*, (29 June 2009), in *Acta Apostolicae Sedis,* 101 (2009), 641-709.

---------, Apostolic Exhortation *Verbum Domini* (30 September 2010), in *Acta Apostolicae Sedis*, 102 (2010), 681-787.

Berger Peter L., "The Desecularisation of the World: A Global Overview", in *The Desecularization of the World. Religion and World Politics,* Peter L. Berger (ed.), Washington, Ethics and Public Policy Centre, 1999, 1-18.

Berridge G.R., *Diplomacy. Theory and Practice*, New York, Palgrave Macmillan, 2010.

Billig Michael, "Prejudice", in *The Social Science Encyclopedia*, Adam Kuper and Jessica Kuper (eds.), London, Routledge, 1985, 641-642.

Boileau A. M., "Etnocentrismo", in *Nuovo Dizionario di Sociologia,* Franco Demarchi, Aldo Ellena e Bernardo Cattarinussi (a cura di), Milano, Edizioni Paoline, 1987, 804-819.

Bordignon Bruno, *Persona è relazione*, Soveria Mannelli, Rubbettino, 2013.

Carrier Hervé, *Dizionario della Cultura per l'analisi culturale e l'inculturazione*, Città del Vaticano, Libreria Editrice Vaticana, 1997.

Cashmore Ellis, "Apartheid", in *Dictionary of Race and Ethnic Relations*, E. Ellis Cashmore, Michael Banton, *et al*, (eds.), London, Routledge, 1988, 18-21.

Conferenza dei vescovi cattolici d'Inghilterra e Galles, "Incontrare Dio nell'amico e nello straniero", in *Il Regno,* Documenti 11 (2010), 358-384.

Congregation for Catholic Education, *Educating to intercultural dialogue in catholic schools: living in harmony for a civilization of love,* Città del Vaticano, Libreria Editrice Vaticana, 2013.

Cordeiro Paola A., Timothy G. Reagan and Linda P Martinez, *Multiculturalism and TQE. Addressing Cultural Diversity in Schools,* California, Corwin Press, 1994.

Corduas Gigliola, "L'interculturalità nei banchi di scuola", in *La Sfida di babele. Incontri e sconti nelle società multicultuirali,* Elena Bein Ricco (a cura di), Torino, Claudina, 2001, 39-66.

*Cultura e Identità in Gioco. Percorsi didattici interdisciplinari di educazione alla pace e al dialogo interculturale,* Maurizio Gusso, Lucia Nadin e Michele Serra (a cura di), Bologna, Editrice Missionaria Italiana, 1995.

De Souza Cyril, "Educazione etico/religiosa in un contesto multireligioso", in *Educare nella Multiculturalità,* Vito Orlando (a cura di), Roma, LAS, 2003, 37-46.

Ellmore R. Terry, *NTC's Mass Media Dictionary,* Illinois, National Textbook Company, 1991.

Fantauzzi Anna Maria, "Razzismo biologico, razzismo differenzialista?", in *Razzismo, xenofobia, esclusione sociale,* Aurelio Angelini (a cura di), Roma, MMXIV Aracne editrice, 2014, 149-172.

Fishman, Joshua A., "Language and Culture", in *The Social Science Encyclopedia,* Adam Kuper and Jessica Kuper (eds.), London, Routledge, 1985, 444.

Francis, Encyclical Letter *Laudato sì* (24 May 2015), Città del Vaticano, Libraria Editrice Vaticana, 2015.

Friedl John, *Cultural Anthropology,* New York, Joanna Cotler Books, 1976.

*Bibliography*

Fromkin Victoria A., "Language", in *The Social Science Encyclopedia*, Adam Kuper and Jessica Kuper (eds.), London, Routledge, 1985, 442-444.

Gennai Giuliana, *Lessico Interculturale*, Bologna, Editrice Missionaria Italiana, 2005.

Hatch Elvin, "Culture", in *The Social Science Encyclopedia*, Adam Kuper and Jessica Kuper (eds.), London, Routledge, 1985,178-179.

Herskovits Melville J., *Man and His Works. The Science of Cultural Anthropology*, New York, Alfred A. Knopf, 1964.

*Human Rights in the Intercultural Dialogue*, Cologne, Konrad Adenauer Foundation, 1998.

*Insegnamenti di Benedetto XVI,* Vol. V parte 1, Città del Vaticano, Libraria Editrice Vaticana, 2010.

*Insegnamenti di Benedetto XVI,* Vol. VI parte 1, Città del Vaticano, Libraria Editrice Vaticana, 2011.

*Insegnamenti di Giovanni Paolo II*, Vol. IV parte 1, Città del Vaticano, Libreria Editrice Vaticana, 1981.

*Insegnamenti di Giovanni Paolo II*, Vol. IX parte 1, Città del Vaticano, Libraria Editrice Vaticana, 1986.

*Insegnamenti di Giovanni Paolo II*, Vol. XVI parte 1, Città del Vaticano, Libraria Editrice Vaticana, 1995.

*Insegnamenti di Giovanni Paolo II*, Vol. XVI parte 2, Città del Vaticano, Libraria Editrice Vaticana, 1995.

*Insegnamenti di Giovanni Paolo II*, Vol. XXIII parte 1, Città del Vaticano, Libreria Editrice Vaticana, 2002.

*Insegnamenti di Giovanni Paolo II*, Vol. XXV parte 1, Città del Vaticano, Libreria Editrice Vaticana, 2004,

International Theological Commission, "Christianity and the World Religions", in *Texts and Documents 1986-2007*, Vol. II, Michael Sharkey and Thomas Weinandy (eds.), San Francisco, Ignatius Press, 2009, 145-186.

International Theological Commission, "Faith and Inculturation", in *Texts and Documents 1986-2007*, Vol. II, Michael Sharkey and Thomas Weinandy (eds.), San Francisco, Ignatius Press, 2009, 1-21.

John Paul II, *Address to UNESCO* (2 June 1980), in *Acta Apostolicae Sedis,* 72 (1980), 735-752.

---------, *Personal Letter to the Cardinal Secretary of State* (20 May 1982), in *Acta Apostolicae Sedis*, 74 (1982), 683-688.

---------, *Speech to the Plenary Session of the Pontifical Council for Culture* (18 January 1983),in *Insegnamenti di Giovanni Paolo II*, Vol. VI parte 1, Città del Vaticano, Libraria Editrice Vaticana, 1983, 147-154.

---------, Apostolic Constitution *"Pastor bonus"* (28 June 1988), in *Acta Apostolicae Sedis,* 80 (1988), 841-900.

---------, Encyclical Letter *Redemptoris missio* (7 December 1990), in *Acta Apostolicae Sedis*, 83 (1991), 249-340.

---------, Motu Proprio *"Inde a Pontificatus"* (25 March 1993), in *Insegnamenti di Giovanni Paolo II*, Vol. XVI parte 1, Città del Vaticano, Libraria Editrice Vaticana, 1993, 747-750.

---------, Encyclical Letter *Veritatis Splendor* (6 August 1993), in *Acta Apostolicae Sedis,* 85 (1993), 1133-1228.

John Paul II, Encyclical Letter *Fides et ratio* (14 September 1998), in *Acta Apostolicae Sedis,* 91 (1999), 5-88.

---------, Apostolic Exhortation *Ecclesia in Asia* (6 November 1999), in *Acta Apostolicae Sedis,* 92 (2000), 449-528.

---------, *"Dialogo tra le culture per una civiltà dell'amore e della pace"*, Messaggio per la celebrazione delle Giornata mondiale della pace (8 dicembre 2000), in *Insegnamenti di Giovanni Paolo II*, Vol. XXIII, parte 2, Città del Vaticano, Libraria Editrice Vaticana, 2002, 1062-1076.

Küng Hans e Kuschel Karl-Josef, *Per un'etica mondiale. La dichiarazione del parlamento delle religioni mondali*, Giovanni Moretto (tr.), Milano, Rizzoli, 1995.

Küng Hans, "Un Confronto fra i due documenti", in *Ethos mondiale e globalizzazione*, Gerardo Cunico, Karl-Josef Kuschel e Domenico Venturelli (a cura di), Genova, Il Melangolo, 2005, 37-42.

---------, *Spurensuche. Die Weltreligionen auf dem Weg*, München, Pieper, 2005.

Lang, G. O., "Culture", in *New Catholic Encyclopedia*, Vol. 4, Washington, Thomson and Gale, 2nd edition, 2003, 426-436.

Luttwak Edward, "The Missing Dimension", in *Religion, the Missing Dimension of Statecraft*, Douglas Johnston and Cynthia Sampson (eds.), Oxford, Oxford University Press, 1994, 8-19.

Mackert Jürgen, "Conflict", in *Encyclopedia of Social Theory*, Austin Harrington, Barbara I. Marshall and Hans-Peter Müller (eds.), London, Routledge, 2006, 90-93.

Menamparampil Thomas, *The Challenge of Cultures*, Bombay, St. Pauls, 1996.

*The New Standard Jewish Encyclopaedia*, Cecil Roth and Geoffrey Wigoder (eds.), Jerusalem, Massada Press, 5th edition, 1977.

Orlando Vito, "L'educazione interculturale: significati e prospettive pedagogiche di realizzazione", in *Educare nella Multiculturalità*, Vito Orlando (a cura di), Roma, LAS, 2003, 95-121;

---------, *Attenzione ai migranti e missione Salesiana nelle società multiculturale d'Europa*, Roma, LAS, 2012.

*L'Osservatore Romano*, 12 marzo 2007, 1.

*L'Osservatore Romano*, 25-26 giugno 2007, 1.

*L'Osservatore Romano*, 2 September 2016, English edition, 2.

*The Oxford English Dictionary*, Vol. 20, Oxford, Clarendon Press, 2nd edition, 1989.

Panikkar Raimon, *Cultural Disarmament. The Way to Peace*, Louisville, Westminster John Knox Press, 1995.

Paul VI, Encyclical Letter *Ecclesiam suam* (6 August 1964), in *Acta Apostolicae Sedis,* 56 (1964), 609-659.

---------, Motu Proprio *"Catholicam Christi Ecclesiam"* (6 January 1967), in *Acta Apostolicae Sedis*, 59 (1967), 25-28.

---------, Motu Proprio *"Apostolicae Caritatis"* (19 March 1970), in *Acta Apostolicae Sedis*, 62 (1970), 193-197.

Pellerey Michele, "Globalizzazione e problemi educativi nella società multiculturale", in *Educare nella Multiculturalità*, Vito Orlando (a cura di), Roma, LAS, 2003, 15-33.

Pettigrew Thomas F. and Taylor Marylee C., "Discrimination", in *Encyclopaedia of Sociology*, Vol. 1, Edgar F. Borgatta (ed.), New York, Macmillan Publishing Company, 1992, 498-503.

Picco Giandomenico, Aboulmagd A. Kamal (*et al*), *Crossing the Divide. Dialogue among civilizations*, New Jersey, Seton Hall University, 2001.

Pontifical Council for Culture, *Towards a Pastoral Approach to Culture,* Città del Vaticano, Libraria Editrice Vaticana, 1999.

*Bibliography*

Pontificio Consiglio per il Dialogo Interreligioso e Congregazione per l'Evangelizzazione dei Popoli, "Dialogo e annuncio: Riflessioni e orientamenti sull'annuncio del vangelo e il dialogo interreligioso" (19 maggio 1991), in *Enchiridion Vaticanum. Documenti Ufficiali della Santa Sede 1991-1993*, Vol. 13, Testo ufficiale e versione Italiana, Bologna, Centro Editoriale Dehoniano, 1995, 191-229.

*Records of the General Conference*, 31st Session, Paris 15 October to 3 November 2001, Vol. 1, *Resolutions*, Paris, UNESCO, 2002.

Roggero L. Dani ed E., "Secolarizzazione", in *Nuovo Dizionario di Sociologia,* Franco Demarchi, Aldo Ellena e Bernardo Cattarinussi (a cura di), Milano, Edizioni Paoline, 1987, 1818-1827.

Rubin Barry, "Religion and International Affairs", in *Religion, the Missing Dimension of Statecraft*, Douglas Johnston and Cynthia Sampson (eds.), Oxford, Oxford University Press, 1994, 20-34.

Seymour-Smith Charlotte, *Macmillan Dictionary of Anthropology*, London, MacMillan, 1986.

Theo Sommer, "Dialog der Kulturen: Von Identität und Integration, Pluralismus und Toleranz", in *Zukunft der Religionen*, Wolfgang Shultheiß (hrsg.), Frankfurt am Main, S. Fischer, 2003, 117-136.

Troyna Barry, "Ghetto", in *Dictionary of Race and Ethnic Relations*, E. Ellis Cashmore, Michael Banton, *et al*, (eds.), London, Routledge, 1988, 118-120.

Tylor Edward. B., *Primitive Culture* [1874], New York, Gordon Press, 2nd edition, 1977.

Ulrich Ralf E., "Migration", in *Encyclopedia of Social Theory*, Austin Harrington, Barbara I. Marshall and Hans-Peter Müller, London, Routledge, 2006, 365-367.

*UNESCO Convention on the Protection and promotion of the Diversity of Cultural Expressions*, Paris, UNESCO, 2005.

Vatican Council II, Pastoral Constitution *Gaudium et spes* (7 Dicember 1965), in *Acta Apostolicae Sedis,* 58 (1966), 1025-1120.

*Webster's Third New International Dictionary of the English Language Unabridged,* Vol. 3, Chicago, Encyclopedia Britannica, 1986.

*White Paper on Intercultural Dialogue "Living Together as equals in dignity"*, Strasbourg, Council of Europe Ministers of Foreign Affairs, 2008.

Winick Charles, *Dictionary of Anthropology*, London, Peter Owen (no date).

Wood Phil and Landry Charles, *The Intercultural City. Planning for Diversity Advantage*, London, Earthscan, 2008.

Zanni Natale, "La scuola in un contesto multiculturale e didattica interculturale", in *Educare nella Multiculturalità*, Vito Orlando (a cura di), Roma, LAS, 2003, 61-67.


**Website materials**

http://anthro.palomar.edu/culture/culture_1.htm (20.5.2017)

http://unesdoc.unesco.org/images/0014/001478/147878e.pdf (1.5.2017)

https://w2.vatican.va/content/francesco/en/speeches/2013/august/documents/papa-francesco_20130821_collegio-saitama-giappone.html (1.5.2017)

*Bibliography*

https://www.scribd.com/document/190875354/Said-Edward-W-The-Clash-of-Ignorance-The-Nation-Article-samuel-huntingtoncivilizations-pdf          (29.12.2017)

# INDEX